Access Now
Behind the Line: The Keys to
Unlimited Possibilities

Access Now
Behind the Line: The Keys to Unlimited Possibilities

Christopher Ivan Franklin

President Gottfried,

Dare to dream!!

Chris
09

URBAN
Renaissance

Urban Books, LLC
1199 Straight Path
West Babylon, NY 11704

ISBN- 13: 978-1-60162-175-7
ISBN- 10: 1-60162-175-2

First Printing August 2009
Printed in the United States of America

10 9 8 7 6 5 4 3 2 1

Distributed by Kensington Publishing Corp.
Submit Wholesale Orders to:
Kensington Publishing Corp.
C/O Penguin Group (USA) Inc.
Attention: Order Processing
405 Murray Hill Parkway
East Rutherford, NJ 07073-2316
Phone: 1-800-526-0275
Fax: 1-800-227-9604

TABLE OF CONTENTS

ACKNOWLEDGMENTS

My sincere thanks to my wife and business partner, Marilyn whose love and dedication motivated me to finish the book. The depth of her wisdom, and creative input throughout the entire process is immeasurable. Thanks goes to my son, Garry for his new school approach in keeping the book real.

I pay tribute to the Titan Financial Services, Inc. clients and its global network. Thank you to my administrative assistant, Scheley Tyler. I thank James Ferguson for his hard work in contributing to the book. Thanks to the focus group for their candid thoughts, which helped to sharpen my skills, and challenge my thinking.

My humble gratitude to my family, friends, and colleagues who encouraged me to forge ahead to complete *Access Now: Behind the Line*. There is no doubt that the "keys to having access to unlimited possibilities is getting beyond the imaginary boundaries in your mind". It is time for you to bring the gear (that's your mind), play the game, and reach your goals.

AUTHOR'S NOTE

Dear Reader:

Some say my rise to the top reads like a storybook. A guy from rural West Virginia becomes President and CEO of his own company, with responsibility for upwards of $100 million of other people's assets. Maybe it is an American classic. But most of you who are reading this book want to live your own success story. And you want it right now!!! I understand how you feel. For too many years that was exactly how I felt. Looking back, I often say to myself, "If I only knew back then what I know now." Maybe I can't go back, but you are in the right place right now. Why? Because I'm going to tell you the things I know now that I wish I knew back then that empowered me to rise to the top of the multimillion-dollar, limited-access sports and entertainment industry. The entire purpose of this book is to give you the keys to achieving your dreams in the future.

Grab the information in this book, study it, apply it, and make it your own. If you do, it will empower you to rise to the top of whatever you choose, wherever you choose to draw your line in the sand. If I did it, you can do it too. Access Now!! Behind the Line: The Keys to Unlimited Possibilities *is going to show you how.*

Christopher I. Franklin
President and CEO
Titan Financial Services, Inc.

PREFACE

I grew up on the outskirts of Charleston, West Virginia, in a small town called Rand. Life was simple in Rand, a town so small that it seemed like everybody knew your name and your parents. That went a long way toward keeping me in check. My siblings and I were blessed with parents who understood the long-term benefits of hard work, good character, and core values. They worked hard to make sure that we grew up with the same understanding. Like most parents, they wanted us to have better lives than they had. One of their goals was for each of us to receive a college degree. The mission was accomplished: three kids, four degrees. Today I know that getting a degree, or two, is not the same thing as getting an education, but I didn't know that then.

From Rand it was off to West Virginia University, where I received a B.S. in accounting, and then on to West Virginia University College of Law. With my freshly minted degrees in hand, the next stop was Houston, Texas, where I had been recruited by a Top 3 accounting firm. It is amazing to me how narrow my thinking was when I arrived in Houston. Like most college graduates, I thought my qualifications were based on my degrees. Eventually I came to the realization that qualifications can never be based on degrees, they can only be based upon skills. I was excited about starting a new job. But I did not even begin to appreciate that I was embarking on a career. Nor did I think to ask whether the short-term job (they are all short-term) was consistent with my long-term goals. Now I can almost laugh and say I was clearly clueless. But it really isn't funny that so many kids are making exactly the same mistakes today.

The management philosophy at the firm was to throw all of the new associates in the fire and see who made it out to the other side. It wasn't fun, but I adapted quickly and rose to the level of Senior Associate. But, more importantly, I grew, and my skill set grew. I developed a much broader perspective on life, the possibilities that life held for me, and my responsibility to make them a reality.

The next and final stop on the job front was Washington, D.C., where I had been recruited to join the emerging sports management industry. My degrees helped to open the door. But the executives that recruited me to go to Washington, D.C. recruited me because they were impressed with the skills I had developed in Houston. Skills that I didn't have when I graduated. I grew and learned a lot while in Houston, but my real education was still just beginning.

Among the many things I learned after arriving in D.C. was not to despise small beginnings. When I started I was the "tax guy." Before it was over, I was a Senior Vice-President of Falk Associates Management Enterprises ("FAME") and ProServ Inc., two of the premier sports management firms of all times (just think *Michael Jordan*). These firms practically, and in some cases literally, wrote the book and the movie on the sports management industry. While I was there I soaked up every bit of information that I possibly could. Then it was time to step out on my own.

It is a huge step to go from collecting a check to creating a check; from being well paid to paying others well. But I took that step and formed Titan Financial Services, Inc. ("Titan"). Titan has carved out its own niche in the multimillion-dollar, limited-access sports and entertainment industry. Today there are few—back then there were even less—men of color who dare to compete *on their own* for the management of financial assets of the rich and famous. Who would have thought that a guy from Rand, West Virginia would ever handle assets in excess of millions of dollars?

Looking back, I can truly say that I enjoyed growing up in West Virginia, and my time at West Virginia University. But despite my appreciation for those times and all of my accomplishments, I still often shake my head and say, "If I only knew back then what I know now." Obviously, there is no way I could know everything that I know now, but coming out of college, knowing a few simple things would have made a huge difference. I wish I had taken more practical courses and acquired more practical skills outside of my academic discipline. Courses and skills in leadership and sales would have been of great help. That alone would have made me more prepared and better equipped to handle the rigors of business and life. I wish I had known that, no matter where you are trying to get to in life, "access" is the end result of a process. Even Oprah Winfrey had to go through a process to become "Oprah." These things are obvious to me now, but if I had known them then, it would have made a huge difference in the amount of time it took me to break through to my current level of success.

Inevitably, it seems that whenever I am interviewed or speaking with emerging leaders, their focus is on my successes. But not everything that has shaped my life shows up on my college degrees, client list, career profile, or even in my total assets under management. I am talking about the things that, to me, are truly priceless: spiritual devotion; my marriage to my beloved wife and business partner, Marilyn; my son Garry; family and close friends who have my best interest at heart; and my health—the foundation that makes everything else work, and without which nothing else seems worth it.

Maybe it is true that the only constant in life is change. It is definitely true that the more comfortable you are with change, the more comfortable and successful your life will be. Change usually shows up as something we are unaccustomed to. For this reason, it is not enough to simply step outside of our comfort zone every time we have an opportunity to do so, because the spot where discomfort and opportunity intersect is where real learning takes place.

Most of the barriers to learning, achieving, and accepting change exist in the mind. I consistently challenge myself to turn those barriers into stepping-stones to greater success. As an advisor to individuals with high net worth, I routinely rub shoulders with the rich, the famous, and the powerful. That is within my comfort zone. But, seeking to expand that zone, I had to humble myself and seek advice from my son on how to connect with a young audience of his college peers.

I attacked other barriers in my mind by riding in a Cigarette boat (a really fast speedboat), interacting with the dolphins in their habitat, and riding in a 50-passenger submarine off into the deep blue, no small accomplishment for a guy who could not swim. The lessons I've learned in the process have been invaluable. Most importantly, I've become accustomed to breaking barriers.

My leisure and professional travels have afforded me an opportunity to observe some truths. One such truth is that we live in a "microwave society" in which people want it all, and they want it all right now. New entrants to the workforce want glitz, glamour, promotions, and power within the blink of an eye, while those who have been in the workforce too often are hesitant, if not reluctant, to re-tool their skills to meet the ongoing technological changes and advances.

For many kids and adults, laptops, the Internet, email, TiVo, text messaging, cell phones, and video games are technological bling. These new technologies, at best, are tools and can never serve as substitutes for thought. As I said in a speech to a group of high school students, "A lot depends on how you use the tools of this high-tech society. Picasso did not use his paintbrush for things that were not productive in developing his skills."

My heart's desire in writing *Access Now* was for others to learn from my mistakes. The things I wish I knew back then are between the covers of this book, and will determine whether you live a life of feast or famine.

The keys provided, all of which are universally applicable, are based on discoveries I have made through trial and error, and what I have learned from others.

The mindset, perspectives, and skills that will inure to the readers of this book are specific but not static, and are just as relevant to the CEO as it is to the trainee; the teacher as it is to the student; the baby boomer and the "echo boomer" (people born between 1978 and 2000); those who know where they are going; and those who are still trying to find out where to go. The book itself is an outgrowth of years of tutoring, teaching, cheering, and encouraging, the touchstones of my commitment to my clients.

Access Now provides the crucial components necessary for success in today's competitive marketplace. It meets you where you are in life. What "line" are you standing behind in your life? *Access Now* reflects the dual realities of "must win now" that we all face daily, and the long-range vision needed to navigate through the processes necessary to secure our future.

What's keeping you from conquering the barriers that stand in your way? How can you turn these barriers into steppingstones to your personal and professional goals? These are the questions you must address to gain access now. See you at the top!!!!

FRANKLIN KEY NUMBER 1: <u>*SELF-LEADERSHIP IS THE PATH TO GREATNESS*</u>

We have to learn to lead ourselves.
—Gloria Steinem (quoted in *Profiles of Female Genius*, 323)

Those who command themselves command others.
—William Hazlitt (quoted in *Believe and Achieve*, 114)

In order to accomplish or to lead anything worthwhile, you must first lead yourself. A drowning man cannot save another. The airline safety instructions always tell you to put on your own mask before helping someone else with theirs. Abraham Lincoln said that you cannot help the poor by being one of them (quoted in *Maximum Achievement*, 24). Margaret Thatcher said that no one would have heard of the Good Samaritan if he only had good intentions. The Bible says that when the blind leads the blind both fall into the ditch (Matthew 15:14). True greatness is too big to be achieved alone. To achieve true greatness you must lead others. In order to lead others you must first lead yourself.

To lead a bad or mediocre team all you need are followers. To lead a great team you must lead leaders. Leading leaders leads to greatness. But we attract what we are, not what we want, and strong leaders will not voluntarily follow weak leaders. So if you don't like the followers you are attracting, you must become a better leader. The key to becoming a leader of leaders is not to seek followers, but to become the type of person others want to follow.

All victory begins with victory over self. All victory requires leadership. To lead, you must read. Continuous forward progress requires continuous input of new information, upon which decisions are made to go left, right, straight ahead, or to make a U-turn if necessary. Seek to learn something from everything and everyone everywhere. Assess yourself. Time is an irreplaceable commodity. Benjamin Tregoe says that the very worst use of time is to do something well that need not be done at all (quoted in Tracy, 17).

The first step toward a chosen destination is to determine where you are. To lead yourself, you must know yourself. Philosopher Lao-tzu called knowing yourself true wisdom. When you do not know yourself, you become subject to the opinions of others who may have neither your best interest at heart, nor your chosen destination or goal in mind. Even if they are well-intentioned, you cannot filter their comments/directions through your own knowledge if you don't know where you are. Many well-intentioned people have wasted significant portions of their lives because they failed to take the time to learn their strengths and weaknesses. To use time wisely you must take steps to operate in your strengths, while minimizing, improving, or at least compensating for your weaknesses.

1. *Assess yourself*

   Unless you correctly identify your current situation, you cannot identify what you need to do to get from where you are to where you want to be. If you are in a hole and your goal is to get to the mountaintop, your top priority should probably be to STOP DIGGING!!! This may seem obvious, but it is only so if you acknowledge/know that you are in a hole. That is why it is crucial that you be totally honest ("brutally honest," "intellectually honest," "real," or whatever you choose to call it), with yourself. If you can't be honest with yourself, find someone who can be honest with you about you. Identify your strengths, your skills, your weaknesses, proclivities, mental outlook, and life philosophy. If you don't like what you find, great!! Why great? Because determined discontent (or, as some might say, necessity) has served as a catalyst for great achievement for women and men throughout the ages. Remember that where you are is a temporary situation, not a permanent condition.

2. *Develop your priorities*

   Success is the end result of going through a process. The greatest success comes only when you focus on what really matters. Activity should not be confused with accomplishment. To the extent you are not working on your number one priority, you are, relatively speaking, wasting time. Do not waste your time. Invest your time. Set a goal to get better every day. Then get better every day. If you continually invest in yourself, the inevitable result is growth, and the end result will be your greater self.

Remember, *Franklin Key Number 1: Self-Leadership is the Path to Greatness.*

Becoming a self-leader requires mastering six more keys:

Franklin Key No. 2:	*Play Your Game*
Franklin Key No. 3:	*A Vision*
Franklin Key No. 4:	*A Decision*
Franklin Key No. 5:	*Sacrifice*
Franklin Key No. 6:	*Personal Development*

The first six keys will attract success beyond what most people realize is available for them. But if you want to achieve greatness, you must master one more key. You must take the step from success to:

Franklin Key No. 7:	*Significance*

I know of no more encouraging fact than the unquestionable ability of man to elevate his life by conscious endeavor.
—Henry David Thoreau (quoted in *Live Your Dreams*, p. 62)

THE FRANKLIN KEYS TO UNLIMITED POSSIBILITIES

1. Self-Leadership is the Path to Greatness

To achieve success you must lead others. In order to lead others you must first lead yourself. Self-leadership requires: Playing Your Game; A Vision; A Decision; Sacrifice; and Personal Development. To move from mere success to true greatness requires *Significance*.

FRANKLIN KEY NUMBER 2: <u>PLAY YOUR GAME</u>

Am I running my race or somebody else's?
—Marlo Thomas

Only the independent thinker will dare to reach for the greatness that will separate them from the masses.
—Christopher I. Franklin

What is the game? Monopoly? Video and internet games? A presidential campaign? A beauty contest? The game is different for everyone. It is simply the challenge you face, and/or the process leading to the goal you want to achieve. Victory is always in the eyes of the beholder. However you define victory, here is how to identify and play your game.

Challenge the Status Quo

What the heck is a *google*? If you follow cricket, you're familiar with a googly. If you're a mathematics geek, you're familiar with a googol. But a *google?* The business headlines will tell you that google is a noun. That it is the name of a financial juggernaut that has surpassed Wall Street earnings expectations in seven of the past eight quarters. The millions of daily users who rely on Google's ubiquitous box will tell you that google is a verb, meaning search, as much as Xerox once meant, to copy. Although Google was recently added to Merriam-Webster's online dictionary, unlike most American-English words, it has no roots in any Romance language. Its roots are deeply imbedded in the language of the American dream, in the language of the universal dream of those for whom a job is not enough, and of those who seek to make their vision a reality by leveraging the power of the World Wide Web.

Google co-founder Larry Page has often said that when he was in college he learned to have a healthy disregard for the impossible (Vise and Malseed, 11). This suspension of disbelief and the refusal to accept so-called boundaries, an operational view that has served the company well, continue to thrive within Google today.

Before Google, search was viewed as generic and undifferentiated. Google broke convention and vaulted to the top of the market because its founders focused solely on running a better search. Providing the best possible response to a search request may be a no-brainer today, but this wasn't the majority view before Google exploded onto the scene and became a financial and social colossus. Google's co-founders, Sergey Brin and Larry Page, turned search into a brand with significant value.

The major players of the pre-Google days, Yahoo, Excite, AltaVista, Infoseek, among others, along with several venture capital firms, declined the opportunity to buy Google for approximately $1 million, even though they realized Google had a demonstrably better product. Google couldn't even get a licensing deal. How shortsighted was this? The day Google went public, its two co-founders became billionaires and they were not yet thirty-two years old. Their view was the unconventional view, but it paid off in a very big way.

Their maniacal focus on search is not the only way that the "Google Guys," as *Playboy* magazine referred to them (Vise and Malseed, 187) in an article that caused Google many problems, have played the game their own way.

Most Initial Public Offerings (IPO's) are dictated by Wall Street. The underwriter advises and dictates the size and the price of the offering. Google dictated the size of its IPO and held an auction to determine the price. Underwriting firms usually pre-sell the intentionally underpriced IPO shares to favored investors, enabling them to profit right away. Google allowed retail investors with only enough money to buy as little as five shares the same access to its IPO as the investors favored by Wall Street. Understandably, underwriters dictate their fees, usually about six or seven percent of the offering's value. In their book, *The Google Story,* authors David A. Vise and Mark Malseed report that Google paid its underwriters less than half of their usual fees (190).

But Google doesn't go its own way simply to be contrarian. Their unorthodox approach has made them extremely successful by any measure. One example is their approach to advertising fees. Businesses usually tell prospective advertisers how much it will cost to post an ad. Google has turned that paradigm on its head by running a continuous automated auction for prospective advertisers to submit bids for ads. But even the highest bid doesn't guarantee a spot. Google factors bid amounts with ad popularity, to determine which ad gets the top spot next to the response to a search request. Although unorthodox, this unusual process makes business sense, since the more people click on an ad, the more money Google makes.

Without question the Google phenomenon has not been without missteps. Missteps are part and parcel of the success process. But the key, as Google VP Marissa Ann Mayer wrote in an article for *Business Week Online*, is "to discover failure fast and abandon it quickly." Google's willingness to risk failure, challenge the status quo, and plot its own course allow it to consistently push through to new levels of discovery and success, making it a worldwide phenomenon.

Having a minority view doesn't mean you have the wrong view. To be successful you may often have to chart your own course in order to break through to higher levels of success. When you do, those who follow the status quo will always tell you that you are going the wrong way. They said the same thing to Google.

Make Up Your Own Mind

Businessman Harland Stonecipher is famous for saying that the most important sale you ever make is the one you make to yourself (King and Robinson, 277). So, before you can play your own game, you must make up your own mind. Life is too short to wear somebody else's tennis shoes. If you chase two rabbits, both will escape. And if you spend part of your time trying to fulfill somebody else's dream for your life, and part of your time trying to fulfill your own dream for your life, you are likely to accomplish neither.

Nobody is better at being you than you, but to be the best you that you can be, to achieve success and happiness, in the words of author John Maxwell, you must "specialize in your specialty" (*17 Essential Qualities of a Team Player*, 86). Your power lies in identifying your dream and never letting go. No one is immune to making mistakes, but if you do find yourself living somebody else's dream, turn around and get back to your dream and onto your road to success. That is what Michael Jordan did.

Michael Jordan is one of the greatest basketball players of all time. In a span of eight years he won six NBA championships. Every year his team won the NBA championship, he was named the Most Valuable Player of the NBA finals. His was the face of the NBA, and traveling with him was like traveling with a rock star. Millions celebrated when he won his third consecutive NBA championship. Millions mourned when his father was tragically and senselessly killed shortly thereafter

11

during a robbery. Several weeks after his father's death, he retired from the NBA to fulfill his father's dream of him playing Major League Baseball.

It is easy to understand why Michael Jordan left the NBA to play professional baseball. Many people pursue careers not of their choosing, to please others. But in addition to loving his father, Michael Jordan also loved baseball. At age 12, he was named "Mr. Baseball" in the state of North Carolina. Despite his love for the game, and even though he was an athlete of great prowess, Michael Jordan never made it to the major leagues. Baseball wasn't his game. His game was basketball.

Michael Jordan returned to the NBA and won three more consecutive NBA championships. Before it was over, his accomplishments included six championships; five NBA MVP awards; three NBA All-Star MVP awards; two Olympic gold medals; and being named one of the 50 Greatest Players in NBA history.

In the game of life, whose game are you playing? If you are not playing your game, you are playing somebody else's game. When you play somebody else's game, you are not likely to win. If you want to win, you've got to make up your own mind and run your own race. You might not immediately vault to the front of the pack, but remember, the race is not always to the swift but to the one that keeps running.

Nowhere is that **principle** more evident than in the post presidential life of Jimmy Carter. Former president of the United States Jimmy Carter has never been known as a trendsetter. He was much more likely to be described as boring and uninspiring. But since leaving office, he has created a new paradigm for the responsibilities, domestic and international, of former presidents.

Even his most ardent supporters would not find it unreasonable to hear Jimmy Carter's single term as president described as turbulent. It was haunted by double-digit inflation; tripling oil prices; long gas lines; unemployment rates over 7%; interest rates over 20%; and the nightly reminder of 52 Americans held hostage for more than a year. The predictable public dissatisfaction ultimately manifested itself in an electoral rout that removed him from office. But even at that challenging time, Jimmy Carter was unwavering in his commitment to peace and human rights.

At the beginning of his presidency, during his inaugural address he spoke of human rights. The high point of his presidency was the signing of the Camp David Accords. The negotiations leading to these agreements, formally known as "*A Framework for Peace in the Middle East*" and "*A Framework for the Conclusions of a Peace Treaty between Egypt and Israel,*" were driven by his desire for peace in the Middle East, and for the preservation of the human rights of Palestinians.

The low point of his presidency was probably the Iranian hostage crisis. Even here he was initially applauded as he chose restraint and peace over retaliation and war. And at the end of his presidency, during his farewell address, again he spoke of human rights. These were the cornerstones of his presidency.

They were also the cornerstones for the unparalleled success of his post-presidency. A success that was fully acknowledged on December 10, 2002 when he was awarded the Nobel Peace Prize for "... his decades of untiring effort to find peaceful solutions to international conflicts [and] to advance democracy and human rights ..." No former president of the United States has had the global impact of Jimmy Carter.

The Constitution of the United States does not provide an official role for former presidents. For most of the later presidents, the opening of the Presidential Library has served as the high watermark of their post-presidency.

Not so for Jimmy Carter. He has raised the bar. Instead of simply building another library where people could conduct research and talk about what happened, the Carter Center makes things happen. It has become a catalyst for advancing peace and human rights throughout the world. It has dispatched 47 international election-monitoring delegations and engaged in the mediation of political disputes, civil wars, and transitions of power, in hot spots all over the world, including North Korea, Bosnia, Haiti, and Venezuela.

Over half of the Carter Center programs are devoted to health efforts, because the Carter Center believes health is a human right. Their work has taken them to 65 of the poorest countries in the world, tackling diseases such as guinea worm and river blindness. The Carter Center also has agricultural programs because they believe that access to food is a human right.

Many Americans are aware of President Carter's work with Habitat for Humanity, probably the smallest part of his work, but it is a very important symbol that fosters the understanding of housing as a human right.

Most of the world agrees that freedom from oppression is a human right. To this end, former President Carter has been directly responsible for the release of more than 50,000 political prisoners.

President Carter's commitment to human rights has not always resulted in immediate success or smooth sailing. In the face of criticism from political opponents, he has taken on diplomatic missions for his successors from both sides of the political aisle, but he has not allowed the opinion of others to sway his beliefs. He often quotes his high school teacher for having taught him, "We must adjust to changing times and still hold to unchanging principles" (Thomas, 45). Jimmy Carter held on to the principle of human rights. As a result, he has achieved a level of global influence unsurpassed by that of any former president of the United States.

Change Is a Part of the Game

Playing your game doesn't mean that you never change. In fact, no matter what your game is, change is an inevitable part of it. Sometimes change is evolutionary, like a business person adjusting to changing consumer tastes. Sometimes change is radical, like moving to a new job or city. But whether change is evolutionary or radical, people who fail to change will find themselves falling farther and farther behind. Others will suddenly find themselves on the outside looking in. Which is what happened to Steve Jobs of Apple.

Steve Jobs was not simply just another businessman or CEO, he was the Bill Gates of the era "before Bill Gates became Bill Gates." He was the first of the young techie millionaires before the dot.com boom exploded through the floodgates. His company, Apple, was the Google of its day, and many of the personal computer companies that followed in the wake of Apple only received venture capital funding because of Apple's success. When Apple sold its shares to the public, it was the most successful IPO in history. Apple was so influential, its founders were awarded the very first National Medal of Technology by President Ronald Reagan.

Steve Jobs was brash, driven, determined, aggressive, and passionate. Charismatic and abrasive, he was a loner who led by force of personality, and a whirlwind who wouldn't take no for an answer. You either rolled with him, or you got rolled over by him. This combustible mix of strengths and contradictions enabled him to take Apple from an idea to a Fortune 500 company in less than five years; made him a millionaire at 24; gave him a net worth of over $200 million by age 25; and, by age 30, got him kicked out of his own company, of which he was chairman of the board.

What happened? Change! Or maybe a better description would be, Jobs's refusal to change. His failure to understand what got him there couldn't keep him there. But don't shed any tears for Steve Jobs. Although he may not be as well known to the general public as he once was, he probably touches more lives now than ever before.

After his departure from Apple, Jobs founded Pixar Animation Studios Inc. Pixar has created some of the most successful animated films of all times: *Toy Story, Toy Story 2, A Bug's Life, Monsters, Inc., Finding Nemo,* and *The Incredibles.* They were smash box office hits with successful second lives on DVD. *Finding Nemo* sold 8 million copies on the very first day it was available on DVD. Pixar's IPO, which took place one week after the release of *Toy Story,* made Jobs a billionaire once again. When the Walt Disney Company purchased Pixar in January of 2006, Jobs became a multibillionaire, the largest Disney stockholder, and a member of its board of directors.

He also regained his seat as Chairman of the Board of Apple and was responsible for moving the Apple iPod from concept to production in one year. Since its introduction in 2001, over 50 million iPods have been sold, and an entire market of peripheral products has sprung up in its wake. Car manufacturers, clothing manufacturers, Burberry, Coach, Gucci, and a host of other companies have all created products specifically for the iPod. Radio stations, colleges (Duke University used to give one to all incoming freshmen), record companies, and even book publishers have been impacted by iPod sales. *Fortune* magazine may have said it best when it described the iPod as a true "cultural and social phenomenon" (Serwer, 2).

Steve Jobs seems to have always had the uncanny ability to paint a picture of the future through I-Technology that was compelling enough to draw even skeptics into his orbit. The problem for those who worked for him, and ultimately for Jobs, was that he always had to be the sun around which everything revolved. Consequently, he was never able to harness the true power of a team. His aversion to anything that didn't evolve around his ideas and his vision was both his strength and his weakness.

In the early days at Apple, Jobs didn't have to adjust. His unwillingness to adapt ultimately caused him problems with both his customers and his shareholders. But he has evolved. Today, Steve Jobs is still demanding, determined, aggressive, charismatic, and a visionary par excellence. He still plays the game his way, but he has changed.

Play The Game To Win

Your job is like that of a contestant on the old game show *What's My Line?*—Guess what the person does for a living. In response to your questions, you've been provided the following information: The contestant speaks English, Russian, French, and Czech; has performed with world-renowned cellist Yo-Yo Ma at his request; had a 136,000-ton supertanker named after them; was told that they didn't have the aptitude for college but received a B.A. *cum laude* by age 19, a master's the following year, and a Ph.D. by age 26; and loves NFL football. What's My Line?

If you said, "The Secretary of State of the United States of America," you are absolutely correct!!!

Dr. Condoleezza Rice became the 66th Secretary of State of the United States of America on January 26, 2005. As Secretary of State, she was fourth in line to succeed the President of the United States, the head of the U.S. Department of State, the chief U.S. diplomat, the chief spokesperson on U.S. foreign policy, and the face of United States interests abroad. She was the first African-American woman, second African-American, and the second woman to reach this pinnacle of U.S. diplomacy.

Prior to being named Secretary of State, Rice served as National Security Advisor from 2001 to 2005, the first female, and the second African-American to hold that position. Earlier she had served six years as Provost of Stanford University. The provost, the second highest position in the university, is the chief academic officer, and is responsible for, amongst other things, administering a budget of over $1 billion. She was the first woman, the first African-American, and, at 38, the youngest person to ever hold the position.

Rice's achievements are stellar. Few people of any sex, race, or nationality can match her credentials. She has set so many firsts, and blazed so many paths, it is often taken for granted. But you do not consistently become the first, the second, the youngest, or the only one to do anything of import by doing things the way everybody else does them. At the very least you have to be determined to do what they do better than they do it, and reject any externally pre-supposed limitations. That is the life philosophy adopted by Condoleezza Rice at an early age, and which sets her apart today. Her story is of crucial importance for those seeking their own path, and for those who feel that the odds are stacked against them, due to sexism, racism, or any other "ism."

The Birmingham, Alabama of Condoleezza Rice's youth has historically served as the poster city for every legal, institutional, social, and pathological "ism" imaginable. It was an environment in which blacks were treated as less than first-class citizens. Parks and public golf courses were closed to prevent desegregation; black-owned homes, businesses, and churches were bombed with impunity and police complicity, and the highest ranking state official blatantly said that a "few first-class funerals" would stop the push for civil rights. The Klu Klux Klan member responsible for using dynamite to blow up a church and kill four little girls in the process, one of them a friend of young Condoleezza, was found guilty of having the dynamite, but innocent of killing the girls who died in the church that he blew up with the dynamite. This sick, wicked, and oppressive environment was the daily reality of those who lived there. Birmingham, Alabama was not an ideal incubator for greatness.

But, in the midst of this, Condoleezza Rice's parents created an environment around her that never allowed those external circumstances to dictate her internal vision of who she could become or what she could accomplish. They didn't allow her to confuse who she was with where she was. And they taught her not to listen to anyone who said, "No, you can't." They had her absolutely convinced, as author Antonia Felix notes in her book, *Condi: The Condoleezza Rice Story*, that even though she "may not be able to have a hamburger at Woolworth's" (36), she could be President of the United States. Having instilled this limitless vision of who she was, and of her horizons, they then set the standard for her work ethic. It was a standard of excellence. It simply required that she be twice as good. Or as *Newsweek* magazine phrased it, the standard required that she "work twice as hard in order to overcome being treated as half a citizen" (Brant and Thomas, 2). And she did.

Playing the game is not always about walking a nontraditional path, walking away from a job or career, or even kicking the door down from the outside. Condoleezza Rice is strategic in her thinking and economical in her movements. She identifies what she wants, thereby making the game her own, and makes every move with that goal in mind. She masters the rules of the system, which allows her to confront it on its own terms. She told one of her professors who espoused the view that blacks were inherently inferior and held back cultural progress, "I speak French, I play Beethoven, I'm better at your culture than you are"(Alva, 2). That short sentence encapsulates her MO. Dr. Condoleezza Rice plays the game from the inside by mastering the rules of the system, and she plays the game to win, or she doesn't play.

Championship Teams

> *The study of mediocrity . . . breeds mediocrity.*
> —Harold Bloom, *Genius*

Championship teams always play to win. Some of the symbols of championship greatness in athletics include the Super Bowl; the World Series; the NBA Championship; the WNBA Championship; the Nextel Cup; the Busch Series; The FedEx Cup; the Majors in Golf; the Majors in Tennis; the World Cup; and many others. Whatever the sport, there is a brass ring that defines greatness. Congress established the Malcolm Baldrige National Quality Award to recognize business excellence. Schools, workplaces, and even cities are recognized in rankings by major business publications. Musicians, actors, actresses, and animators all have specific awards recognizing excellence in their craft, such as the Grammies, the Academy Awards, the BET Awards, and the American Music Awards. Whatever the arena, champions become champions by playing their game.

The Chicago Bulls ran the triangle offense. You knew it was coming; they knew you knew it was coming. But they did it anyway and won three championships in a row. Twice! With Woody Hayes and the Ohio State Buckeyes, it was "three yards and a cloud of dust." They won four outright national championships (one shared), and 13 Big Ten titles. With the Green Bay Packers under Vince Lombardi, it was the Green Bay "sweep." Together they won five NFL championships as well as the first two Super Bowls. Lombardi's name has become so synonymous with greatness, the NFL's most prestigious award is called the Lombardi Trophy. Bill Russell's name has also become synonymous with greatness because he won 11 NBA championships in his 13-year career.

Muhammad Ali during his reign as "the greatest" initiated and, more often than not, won the mind game with his opponents before the fight even began. Opponents foolish enough to play his game lost the psychological battle and the fight itself. They entered the ring mad, and, intent on proving him wrong, were easily flustered. Ali's tactics inside the ring, the rope-a-dope, arguably, the most notable, were an extension of the mind game he started before the fight. His opponents fought his fight and usually lost. Whose fight are you fighting?

From his amateur career through his professional career, Tiger Woods has set numerous firsts on the golf course. He was the youngest to win the U.S. Junior Amateur and the first to win it more than once. He was the youngest to win the U.S. Amateur. He was the first golfer to hold all four major championships at the same time. He was the youngest golfer to be ranked No. 1 on the Official World Golf Ranking. And he has more career victories than any active player. After he blew up the course, and blew away the field at the Masters in 1997, tournaments began reconfiguring courses in an effort to make them "Tiger proof." They started changing the game in order to beat Tiger Woods. They knew they couldn't wait on him to change his game and beat himself.

If you want to win you have to play your game. That's

why a coach tells her team to stick to the game plan, and a cornerman tells the boxer to fight his fight. Often, you hear the term "home court" or "home field" advantage. The team with a home court or home field advantage has an edge, if only psychological. Playing your game also gives you an advantage. Championship teams that play their game, whether in business, sports, or any other aspect of life, have an advantage that increases the likelihood of success.

Opponents in a professional championship game or match are usually closely matched. The team that wins is usually the one that can impose its will on its opponent. The one that can impose its will is the one that plays its game.

Basic Skills for Playing Your Game

It may seem obvious that you cannot impose your will until you know what you want to accomplish, yet this is exactly the sticking point for many well-meaning and hard-working people. They fail to identify exactly what they want to accomplish. This places them at a severe disadvantage to those who do know what they want from an encounter, a job, a school, a relationship, or whatever else they engage in. Typical examples of this common mistake are the couple with great plans for the wedding, but none for the marriage; another couple with a house, but not a home; the person with a job, but no future; and the student with a degree, but no education. Without a goal, you can be neither strategic in your thinking, nor economical in your movement. The absence of a goal is most often evidenced by either no movement and no progress, or a lot of movement but very little progress.

Playing your game is the antithesis of being stagnant in your thinking or close-minded in your approach. Successful people and successful companies are fluid in their thinking, and proactive in their approach. They intentionally adopt an "*avante garde*" student mindset, seek out new information and opportunities, and think through processes so as not to confuse a tool with a goal. The goal is the desired result. The tool is the means to that end. For example, students, routinely use college as a means to a higher-paying job and better lifestyle. Employees in the workplace often move from job to job in search of the same thing. In both cases the "tool" provides access to a different level of success.

Rap and hip-hop was once shunned just as it is embraced today. It grew out of a sub-culture of a culture that was already far removed from the mainstream. It was not only distinctive in sound and dress, but its distance from the mainstream was deemed a core component of its legitimacy. What became known as "gansta rap," and its performers, was fodder for presidential campaigns, and was excoriated in the halls of Congress and in corporate boardrooms. On occasion it was even pulled from store shelves.

But today hip-hop has unquestionably replaced Motown as the signature sound of young America. Rappers and pop performers routinely collaborate. In fact, hip-hop has become so embedded in American culture that one writer refers to it as "hip-pop." Rappers can now be found standing next to members of Congress announcing social initiatives and holding press conferences. The leading rap moguls, including those formerly referred to as "gansta rappers," now wear so many three-piece suits that they are at times indistinguishable from those who formerly excoriated them. Their incomes and business activities are reported in mainstream business publications like *Forbes* and *The Wall Street Journal.* They are presidents of corporate entities, owners of restaurant chains, nightclubs, award-winning clothing lines, and numerous other mainstream businesses. Their endorsements run literally from head to toe, from hats to shoes, and include telephones, chewing gum, video games, health clubs, and sports drinks. They appear in movies with established box office draws, and appear in print and television advertisements, sometimes alone, other times with business icons, such as Lee Iacocca.

This extreme shift in position is not coincidental on the part of the artists or of the corporate entities that now embrace them. It is a direct result of both the artists and the corporate entities playing their game. The artists' superior *processing skills* allowed them to see that hip-hop was a tool, not a goal, a means to an end, not an end in itself. They played their game by using rap and hip-hop to get paid and to open the door to bigger pay-days. Once the doors to bigger paydays opened, their *crossover skills* enabled them to change clothes and walk through the doors. They were able to change clothes, literally and figuratively, because they didn't allow their paradigm to become frozen in time or place, or allow the negative perception that others may have had of them to freeze them in time or place.

The corporate entities are playing their game and are now embracing the artists because the artists influence a significant number of potential customers. Corporate entities and advertisers seek to create an image for themselves in alignment with whom or whatever is "hot" or popular at the moment. When the artist is no longer hot, the corporate entities and advertisers drop them and move on to the current "flavor of the month."

The chameleon-like ability to be "adept at adapting" and to change methods and tools is a hallmark of successful people and businesses. Wayne Huizenga started with one trash truck. He would pick up the trash in the morning, and then he would change clothes and solicit new business in the afternoon. He recognized that he had to fulfill different roles, and present different faces to different customers. Being adept at adapting enabled him to take the business that he started with one truck and turn it into what is now a publicly traded multinational company known as Waste Management, Inc., which is now the lead provider nationally of commercial, residential, and environmental services.

Huizenga has had a tremendous amount of success since starting out with that one trash truck, going on to purchase or create several other well-known businesses, including: AutoNation; Blockbuster Video; Extended Stay America, Inc.; the Florida Marlins, the Florida Panthers; and the Miami Dolphins. He had to adapt to the traditional business practices when he started with one truck. But he has also had to adapt his methods of operation with each new industry he has entered. Notwithstanding the success of his businesses, Wayne Huizenga remains proactive in seeking new opportunities and never views himself in the context of his business affairs. Speaking with a writer for *Fortune* magazine, Huizenga said, "[I] didn't think of myself as being in the waste collection business. I wasn't in the video business. I'm in the moneymaking business" (Martin and Huizenga, 5).

Many people are quick to announce some variation of "I'm in the moneymaking business," but unless they have specifically identified a tangible goal and are directing all of their energy toward achieving that goal, they are fooling themselves. Wayne Huizenga has built three Fortune 1000 companies and six New York Stock

Exchange listed companies. He has clearly and repeatedly identified, and successfully achieved, what he wanted to achieve. But he would never have been able to climb such heights if he'd never envisioned himself climbing out of his trash truck. In 2005 Wayne Huizenga was named the Ernst & Young World Entrepreneur of the Year.

Successful businesses, successful people, and successful students, with the avante garde mindset, utilize the processing, crossover, and adapting skills discussed above to varying degrees. But the one skill that they all use all of the time, probably the most important skill of them all, is their "survival skill." Often we think of survival as just holding on, or barely getting by, but successful people do much more than that.

Survival skills are necessarily varied and situation-specific, but there are some common manifestations. People with survival skills work harder after a victory and seek to harness the momentum, "the push" that comes from success. When things are going well, people with survival skills do not become complacent but remain vigilant for signs of danger. They look ahead at all times, seeking to identify the trends and patterns that may impact them along their path. They think globally, while acting locally, always moving with a bigger picture in mind, and refusing to be the one-trick pony by putting all of their eggs in one basket. People with survival skills never settle, and they always play their own game.

> *This above all: to thine own self be true.*
> —Shakespeare, *Hamlet*

THE FRANKLIN KEYS TO UNLIMITED POSSIBILITIES

2. ***Play Your Game***
    In the game of life, whose game are you playing?
    Playing your game enables you to be strategic in
    your thinking and economical in your move-
    ments. If you are not playing your game, you are
    playing somebody else's game. Rarely is some-
    body else's game created for your benefit. If you
    want to win, if you want to achieve success and
    happiness, you've got to make up your own mind
    and play your game.

FRANKLIN KEY NUMBER 3: ALWAYS MOVE TOWARD YOUR VISION

We believe that each player should plan for his career after the sport while still playing the sport.
—Christopher I. Franklin

When Alice in Wonderland came to a fork in the road, she asked the Cheshire Cat, "Which road should I take?"

"Where are you going?" asked the cat.

"I don't know," said Alice.

"Then it doesn't matter," the cat was quick to reply.

It is hard to feel sorry for a young man who signs a multimillion-dollar contract with the NBA and then blows his chance at a comfortable life. The stories of former millionaire athletes now destitute have become commonplace. Yet, these stories still evoke a sense of sadness. Many readers of these stories under the age of 25 and still lacking an appreciation of their own fallibility are prone to say the athlete was stupid. They find it implausible that they would make a similar mistake. Readers over the age of 40 often think, if only ever so briefly, of opportunities that they have blown.

Athletes are unique, in the sense that they suffer the embarrassment of having their failure broadcast to the entire world, but they are really no different from the lottery winners who end up in financial trouble, those who blow the once-in-a-lifetime job that they always wanted, students who get into great schools and fail to take advantage of the opportunity to get a great education, or the spouse who married the person of his/her dreams and blows the relationship over some "indiscretion." Every situation is unique, but the most common thread that connects these and other similar situations is a lack of vision.

The destitute former athlete who wasted millions, the former student who spent more time having fun than getting an education, and the indiscreet spouse all acted on their desire for immediate gratification. Living for today, with no thought for tomorrow, they did not begin with the end in mind. To begin with the end in mind means to have a vision of your desired end result, a mental roadmap to serve as a guide for your choices. Many people have more of a goal, or a vision, for the desired end of their Saturday night than they do for their lives. When you have a vision for your life, you will measure all that you do on whether it helps you or hurts you in making your vision your reality.

Some people routinely "pimp their rides" because they have a vision of what they want their cars to look like. Others won't drive their cars in certain places because they don't want their cars dirtied, damaged, or stolen. How many people treat their lives as well as these people treat their cars?

If you want to change your life, you must create a vision for your life. The Bible says that the people perish for a lack of vision, and that when the blind leads the blind, both fall into a ditch. To achieve great things, you must begin with a vision of the great thing you want to achieve. Nobody ever fell to the top of the mountain. Success begins with vision.

Vision Determines Destiny

> *The key to having access to unlimited possibilities is getting beyond the imaginary boundaries established in your mind.*
> —Christopher I. Franklin

> *Keep your eyes on the path ahead and your body will usually follow.*
> —Talane Miedaner, *Coach Yourself to Success*

We generally move toward whatever we focus on the most. Whatever we focus on the most, we will think on the most. And "As a man thinketh, so is he" (Allen, 9). Identifying a destination gives you the power of focus. Those who focus on success are likely to succeed. Those who focus on failure are likely to fail.

In order to maximize your power of focus, you must take the time to think through and to develop absolute clarity on where you want to go. It is imperative that you create a vision of your desired end result. That vision is your destination. The simple step of identifying a destination will begin to change your thinking. Changing your thinking will change your choices. It will also change how you view the choices, and even the identities, of those around you.

When you are lost or trying to get somewhere important, you evaluate everything in terms of its impact on where you want to go. Do I have time to watch TV? Do I turn left or right? Do I go straight or turn around? If you are on your way and the people around you are moving too slowly, you look for another path or for a way around them. Identifying a destination for your life, your business, your relationships, your health, your weight, or for anything else will have the same effect. You will begin to see things through the prism of whether it moves you toward, or hinders you from reaching, your destination. If you fail to identify a destination, you will find yourself running with the crowd and going nowhere.

A Vision is Limitless

A vision is powerful. It is framed by the unlimited vista of the human imagination and empowered by the immeasurable power of the human heart. It cannot be limited by the situations or circumstances in which you may find yourself. In fact, the worse your circumstances, the more important it is that you have a vision, and the more power your vision will be capable of unleashing in your life. A vision has the power to lift anyone from the depths of the direst of circumstances to the highest of heights imaginable.

Oprah Winfrey's story is as heart-wrenching as it is awe-inspiring. She was born in 1954 in Mississippi at a time when African-American was not the descriptive term most commonly used for a black person in that region of the country. Born to a single mother from what she describes as a "one-day fling under an oak tree," she lived with a series of family members, beginning with her grandmother, who had no bathroom in the house. By the age of fourteen, she had been raped, ran away from home, and had a miscarriage. At best, the likely end result for anyone forced to begin life under these circumstances is not good. But truth, as is often said, can be stranger than fiction. Today she has an estimated fortune of over a billion dollars.

Oprah did not merely wish to be rich, she resolved to be rich. Her threadbare Horatio Alger nightmare to Gucci wear story shows the power of a vision. Oprah had a vision so powerful, it picked her up despite the circumstances of her youth, which would have chained most people down.

But she is not the only one whose vision moved her from the outhouse to the penthouse. Helen Keller had no sight, but her vision continues to inspire millions. Pharisee Saul lost his sight on the road to Damascus, but he immediately gained a vision that continues to change the world. There are many others, but that is not important. What is important is that now it is your turn. What is your vision?

Vision Begins Within

Both Ralph Waldo Emerson and Oliver Wendell Holmes Sr., father of Supreme Court Justice Oliver Wendell Holmes Jr., have been credited with having said "what lies behind us and what lies before are tiny matters compared to what lies within us." Whoever among these accomplished gentlemen made the statement, the fact is that the biggest potential obstacle and the biggest potential springboard to your success are both within you. Your thoughts and beliefs will serve as either your biggest obstacle or as the biggest launching pad you ever imagined. A vision has nothing to do with how or where others see you. It has everything to do with where you see yourself.

You may not know who Jay Rubin is, but you're probably familiar with some of his work. Frederick Jay Rubin was in many ways the typical Jewish American kid from a comfortable home in Long Island, New York. He grew up listening to and loving the Beatles, AC/DC, and Led Zeppelin, not exactly the expected background for the producer of performers such as Public Enemy, LL Cool J, the Geto Boys, and Jay-Z. And as if that wasn't counterintuitive enough, although he broke through with rap, he also produced acts such as Aerosmith, Slayer, The Red Hot Chili Peppers, Johnny Cash, The Dixie Chicks, and most poetically fitting, Rage Against the Machine. Jay Rubin's vision of himself as a producer of various music genres was not limited by the stereotype others may have had of what he could achieve based on his background. His vision of himself and of his music was in his head, and he has never allowed anybody to take it away. Neither should you.

A Vision Empowers

> *Having sight but no vision is the worst thing that can happen to a person.*
> —Helen Keller

A vision is what helps the helpless get up and keep trying. It is what pushes those who reach the goal to take the last step, the last shot, and the last stretch that results in victory, after they've given their all. A vision is what gives the discouraged courage to keep going despite all the dark clouds on the horizon.

Vision leads the leader. It is the spark that lights the match that lights the fuse that sets off the explosion that blows away every excuse, limit, situation, or condition. Vision fuels the fire within and creates an internal light so bright that everything else pales in comparison. Vision draws the willing forward, it pushes as it pulls and catapults the willing on to new heights, limited only by the willingness of the vision holder to receive.

A Vision Is Magnetic

Identifying a destination gives you the power of magnetism. As like attracts like, you will attract those going where you are going. For better or for worse, you are attracting what you are right now. If you change your vision, you will change who and what is attracted to you. Change your vision and you will change your thoughts, words, choices, actions, and attractions. A vision truly desired and reached for will shape you into the very thing you seek. As you become what you desire, what you desire will come to you. Change your vision and you will change your life.

Like attracts like in every walk of life. Nuns are attracted to the nunnery, and bowlers are attracted to the alley. You've probably heard these truisms so often that you know them by heart: Birds of a feather flock together; Show me your company and I'll tell you who you are. Whether it's a cell group, a rock group, a school of fish, or a school of thought, like attracts like.

A Fortune 500 study found that 94% of all the executives surveyed attributed their success more to attitude than any other factor. Rarely are positive and negative people attracted to each other. Winners have little tolerance for whiners. Those who see opportunity are not disposed to spend much time with those who only see problems. Whatever character you possess, you are likely to find in those closest to you. If you don't like the people around you, don't work harder on changing them, work harder on changing you.

Identifying Your Vision

> *All men dream, but not equally. Those who dream by night in the dusty recesses of their minds awake to find that it was vanity; But the dreamers of day are dangerous men; That they may act on their dreams with open eyes to make it possible.*
> —T.E. Lawrence (Lawrence of Arabia)

To help identify your vision, answer a few questions: What excites you? What is the one thing that, if you could, you would do? What is your dream? What is it that you would become if you knew then what you know now? Many people answer these questions but never move on the answers, because they make excuses for themselves, such as they are too old.

Ray Kroc was over fifty when he launched McDonald's into the most successful franchise in the world. Harland Sanders, better known as Colonel Sanders, was over sixty years old when he started Kentucky Fried Chicken. So what if it will take fifteen years to fulfill your dream? You are going to be fifteen years older in fifteen years anyway. You are far better off being fifteen years older and living your dream than being fifteen years older singing, "If I coulda woulda shoulda." Lou Rawls is the only **person** I know who got paid for singing that song.

What is it that you **know would** change the world, or save lives, or create an industry? Hip-hop is a billion-dollar industry. Rap records did a billion dollars in sales again last year, but there was no hip-hop industry, no history of billion-dollar rap record sales, when Sylvia Robinson created the Sugarhill Gang and released "Rapper's Delight" on her Sugar Hill Records label. There was no Queen Latifah, no TLC, and no Salt-N-Pepa, when Sylvia Robinson signed, recorded, released, and hit with female rap group, The Sequence. Rap had no known social conscience, at least none that sold records, when Sylvia Robinson badgered Sugar Hill artists Grandmaster Flash and the Furious Five until they recorded their seminal hit track, "The Message," which went gold in 21 days.

Sylvia Robinson's Sugar Hill Records was the cradle of the nascent rap industry. She created the blueprint and the environment for the success of other ground-breaking labels, such as Profile Records, Uptown Records, LaFace Records, and Def Jam Recordings. Sylvia Robinson made plenty of mistakes, but the meteoric beginning and inglorious end of Sugar Hill still serves as a great lesson.It may be easy to look back and say what Sylvia Robinson did was a no-brainer, but hindsight is 20/20, whereas a fool is always blind.

Music is a $40 billion global industry dominated by an incredibly small number of multinational conglomerates. They spend millions discovering and/or creating the next big thing. They spend millions more squashing anything that threatens their control over what is sold, and where it gets played. They maintain a chokehold over distribution. The folks at Napster could attest to this, if there are any of them left. Sylvia Robinson got it done. Despite the odds, and so can you.

Whatever your ultimate goal may be, that is your

dream. The dream is the precursor to the vision. To achieve greatness in any area of your life, be it spiritual, physical, financial, business, or personal, you must be a dreamer, a visionary. Among high achievers, studies have shown that those who dream the most achieve the most. The dream is the seed, the acorn, from which the concomitant power and oak-like majesty of every vision is derived. Every dream will not result in a vision, but where there is no dream, there can be no vision.

If your vision is murky, or if you just don't have a vision of your own, don't panic. Begin your search by simply looking at what is going on around you. There aren't any special points for originality. In his book, *The Billion Dollar BET*, author Brett Pulley points out that Bob Johnson got the business plan for BET by copying, with permission, the business plan for an over-50 TV channel someone else was trying to get up and running (33). Bob Johnson is now a billionaire and owns an NBA franchise. Have you heard of anyone who has gotten rich from the over-50 channel? Have you ever heard of the over-50 channel?

The old line goes, if you build a better mousetrap, the world will beat a path to your door. It does not say you have to think of it first. You don't even have to build it first. Betamax came first, but got crushed by VHS. There were many other coffee shops before Starbucks, hardware stores before Home Depot, and discount stores before Wal-Mart. But today Starbucks, Home Depot, and Wal-Mart reign supreme as the undisputed leaders of their industries.

If you see someone else whose vision moves you, join

forces with them. Eagerly assist that person in fulfilling their vision. You've heard the stories and you've seen the movies about the water boy that became the star, the understudy that stepped in for the diva, and the mail clerk that became CEO. So don't despise small beginnings.

In the beginning Spinderella was the DJ that replaced the DJ for fledging female rappers, Salt-N-Pepa. Before it was all over, Salt-N-Pepa was one of the few hip-hop artists to have a long-term career, and Spinderella was sharing top billing. Spinderella was also doing solo projects with traditional pop and R&B artists such as Luther Vandross. She appeared as a guest on numerous shows outside of the rap mainstream, such as *Late Night with David Letterman* and *The Tonight Show*. In the beginning, maybe Spinderella was there in support of someone else's vision, or maybe because it was one of the necessary steps in her quest to fulfill her own vision, but whatever the reason, she made her vision a reality. So can you.

Andre Harrell made $200 a week as a Vice President for Def Jam Recordings. In Texas they call that "big hat, no cattle." A few years later, Uptown Entertainment was formed as a joint venture between Def Jam and MCA. Fast forward several more years and you will find that Mr. Harrell sold his stake in Uptown Entertainment for more than $30 million when he took over Motown Records. I don't know what they call that in Texas, but it would seem safe to say that "big hat, no cattle" no longer fit, because now he has a big title and big money.

While a student at Howard University, Sean "P. Diddy"

Combs started out as an intern at Uptown under the mentorship of Andre Harrell. Today he is the head of a multimillion-dollar empire, which includes a music label, an award-winning clothing line, and a chain of restaurants. He made *Fortune* magazine's list of "40 Richest People Under 40." His current estimated net worth is over $300 million.

Your goal may not be to make music or to make millions, but it doesn't matter, because the principles of success are still the same. So remember: don't despise small beginnings.

Focus Your Vision

1. *Be God-Focused*

Stop every day to look at the size of God. Most people spend most of their lives looking at the perceived size of their problem. Take time every day to consider God's greatness and decide to believe His promises for greatness in your life.

2. *Be Result-Focused*

Winston Churchill once said, "It is not enough that we do our best; sometimes we have to do what's required." Anytime you concentrate on the difficulty of the work instead of its results or rewards, you're likely to become discouraged. The man who walks around with his head down may find some loose change, but he'll never find new heights. Focus on your goals, not on your problems.

3. *Be Relationship-Focused*

Dedicate yourself long term to the process of relationship building. Look past what you can receive to what you can give, and watch your relationships blossom. A relationship should be treated like a fragile plant. It is to be nourished, maintained and placed in the best possible light for it to grow. In due season, the young sapling you were able to hold in one hand when you planted it will become a mighty oak in which you can build a tree house. Take the long view toward relationships. In the beginning it may seem that you give more than you receive. In the end you will receive much more than you ever gave.

All getting separates you from others; all giving unites to others—St. Francis of Assisi (quoted in *17 Essential Qualities of a Team Player,* 129)

4. *Be Development-Focused*

Take charge of your personal growth. Don't confuse where you are as a result of short-term events with who you are. But do note the dominant pattern of results, circumstances, relationships and conditions in your life. The external patterns are direct reflections of your internal personal development. To improve your life, you must improve yourself. To change your external reality, you must change your internal reality.

Personal development is cumulative. Reading twenty minutes a day may seem like a small thing, but the progress you will make over time will be life-changing. Try saving a penny and doubling the total amount saved every day for thirty days. On day one you will have the penny. On day two you will have two cents. On day three you will have four cents. On day thirty you will have several million dollars!!! (I'll wait until you are finished with the calculator.)

5. *Be Character-Focused*

You must walk the talk. You might fool somebody else temporarily, but you won't fool you. Business philosopher Jim Rohn said, "Judas got the money, but he threw it all away and hung himself because he was so unhappy with himself." It may help to remember that. Place emphasis on values, standards, integrity, and morality.

6. *Be Vision-Focused*

Have a laser-like focus and tenacity to see the vision through to completion.

Bling Blurs Vision

Thousands upon thousands are yearly brought into a state of real poverty by their great anxiety not to be thought poor.
—William Cobbett, *Advice to Young Men*

The power of bling transcends gender, race, and class. Consumption mindedness, the mistress, the cars, the gold, the ice, the crib, the clothes, the shoes; and more flash than substance, all comprise normal excess for today's professional athlete without a vision for their future. Consumption mindedness, the mistress; the car note that is higher than the rent, the gold, the excessive drinking to prove "manhood," the foul mouth to prove street credibility, the cutting classes, the clothes, the shoes, the electronic trinkets, the weekly trips to the nail and hair salon that cost an absurd amount of an already limited disposable income; and more flash than substance, all comprise normal excess for those that have neither millions to spend nor a vision for their future.

Clearly, there is very little difference between the athlete and the non-athlete. It's all bling, and it ain't all good. Bling reflects a mindset that image and consumption is king.

Most of the people you are trying to impress are going to leave you in the end, even though they probably had even less than you did in the beginning. Millionaire athletes buy toys to impress their "boys," many of whom generally do not have a pot to piss in or the window to throw it out of. What a waste! People with substance don't think those foolish enough to waste their money on baubles are cool. They know they are fools. But yet, lives, and untold millions are wasted in an effort to impress those who don't matter or don't care. " 'Beam me up, Scotty!!' "

Bling focuses on what you appear to be, but vision focuses on where you want to be. Bling, at its core, is an external trinket being used to fix an internal problem. A Band-Aid will not stop internal bleeding.

Those who have been blinded by the power of bling continue to purchase more and more at the cost of their future financial security. Instead of seeing bling as a trap, a wish or desire, they see it as a necessity. Instead of seeing it as a temporary distraction or the reward at the end of a process, bling for them is a goal in and of itself. In the military there is something called a PX soldier. PX soldiers are military personnel who go to the PX (post exchange/military store) and buy military gear reflecting various accomplishments that they have not earned. Bling is similar. It is used to falsely signal to others that you have arrived at a place, most often financial, that in reality you have not.

When you are blinded by bling, bling becomes king. When bling becomes king, it shifts your focus from your greater objective (being able to maintain your lifestyle after you retire) into a series of unproductive short-term goals (looking good in the Benz) without any long-term value (which would keep you from spending your golden years at the golden arches). It undermines financial strategies by diverting limited resources to unconstructive use. Bling ultimately destroys "the best laid plans of mice and men," moving misplaced priorities to the fore, and life-defining objectives to the abyss of good intentions. When bling is king, your ego gets between you and your objectives, and you become your own worst enemy.

Moving Beyond Bling

> *We hold these truths to be self-evident: that all*
> *men are created equal; that they are endowed by*
> *their creator with certain inalienable rights; that*
> *among these are life, liberty and the pursuit of*
> *happiness.*
> —The Declaration of Independence

To move beyond bling, you must lead yourself and manage your life. Moving beyond bling does not mean that you have to live a life with no toys, no freedom, and no happiness. Life with no toys would, at best, be mere existence. However, in a life where bling is king, you will find yourself stuck in a perpetual rut, unable to move forward, and inevitably fall backwards. Being stuck in a rut is not liberty. A life where bling is king will result in being trapped in a world of debt and bondage, making it harder to pursue happiness. But working 40 years for a gold watch to retire on 60% of what wasn't enough when you had 100% of it is not the pursuit of happiness either. To enjoy life, liberty, and the pursuit of happiness, you must move beyond bling, leading yourself and managing your life.

Amazingly, most of us have more understanding of the rules for managing the games we play than the rules for managing the lives we live. The playground game for deciding who got the ball used to be odds and evens. Elsewhere, it was rock, paper, and scissors. These methods of decision-making are so well-established, kids from different parts of the world can come together on the playground and agree on how to get things done. Which leads to the question, if paper covers rock, and scissors cut paper, what trumps bling? Apply the following steps in every aspect of your life, and you will be well on your way to trumping bling and successfully running your own race in business and in life:

Self-assessment	- Determine where you are
Identify the goal	- Know where you want to go (Vision)
Create a plan	- Map out the path
Exercise self-control	- Stay on the path (Make goals definite, but keep methods flexible)
Be committed	- Measure contemplated actions by their alignment with your goals
Check your progress	- If I keep doing what I am doing, will I end up where I want when I want? Have circumstances changed, necessitating a change in plans?

Commit to a vision for your career, your finances, your relationships, your relationship with God, and your health. In the presence of vision, life's purpose grows. Your vision determines the tree upon which to rest your ladder of success. The plan is the rungs leading to the top of the ladder. No one is responsible for your success but you. No one can climb your ladder but you. Often, especially in the beginning, no one can see the tree upon which your ladder rests but you. When you commit to your vision, you will avoid the pitfalls of a life in which bling is king, and you will achieve the heights to which you dare to dream.

Challenge Your Excuses

If you don't know how to do something [that is worth doing], it is worth doing badly until you learn to do it well.
—Les Brown, *It's Not Over until You Win*

Nobody who drives a car waits until all the lights are green before leaving home. But in seeking to create the future we desire, we often think of all the reasons why we can't do something and allow them to prevent us from even starting. You can either choose to live your dreams, or you can choose to live your excuses. Few people choose to live their dreams; most people choose to live their excuses. Most excuses lay blame for our circumstances or our choices on something or someone outside of our control. To the extent we place responsibility outside of ourselves, we give up control of our ability to change our circumstances. An African proverb says, "He who cannot dance will say the drum is bad." Don't choose your excuses, challenge them. The extent to which you challenge your excuses is the extent to which you take control of your life. And when you take control of your life, you are free to choose your future.

Your ability to achieve is not fixed by where you are not, nor by what you know. Your ability to achieve is only limited to the extent you refuse to let go of the past, embracing the present, and creating the future. Do not let your past determine your future. Where you are today is a result of decisions made yesterday. If in the past you decided to be a couch potato, your present physical body reflects that decision. Don't let that stop you from deciding to build the body you want. If in the past you dropped out of school, don't let that stop you from getting the education you want. Old decisions are just that, old decisions. Let the past pass. Now make new decisions for your new direction.

The difficulty lies not in the new ideas but in escaping from the same old ones.
—John Maynard Keynes (quoted in O'Loughlin, 41)

Celebrate Your Vision

> *Aerodynamics have proven that the bumblebee*
> *cannot fly. The body is too heavy and the wings are*
> *too weak. But the bumblebee doesn't know that*
> *and it goes right on flying*
> *miraculously.*
> —Mary Kay Ash (quoted in Gross, 233)

Your vision is uniquely your own. Celebrate uniqueness. Your uniqueness will sometimes mean you'll have to
stand alone. A leader often stands alone. Your uniqueness
will sometimes distinguish you from the crowd. The few
who are leaders will always stand out amongst the masses,
or followers.

Your uniqueness will sometimes cause you to see
things differently from others. The view from the front
is always different from the view in the middle of the
pack. Your uniqueness will sometimes cause you to pay
a price, or lose a "friend." Leadership carries a price (for
everything else there is MasterCard) that few are willing
to pay.

Your uniqueness will sometimes make you subject to
different treatment. Well, the taller the tree, the greater
the pressure from the storms. Your uniqueness means
that you may be dancing to the beat of a different
drummer. Good for you. Enjoy the dance.

ACCESS NOW BEHIND THE LINE

THE FRANKLIN KEYS TO UNLIMITED POSSIBILITIES

3. *Always Move Toward Your Vision*
To achieve great things, you must begin with a vision of the great thing you want to achieve. This empowers you to see things through the prism of whether it moves you toward, or hinders you from achieving, your dreams. It doesn't matter if achieving your dreams is going to take fifteen years. You are going to be fifteen years older in fifteen years anyway. Success begins with a vision.

FRANKLIN KEY NUMBER 4: <u>MAKE A DECISION</u>

To be successful in America you need only two things: First, decide exactly what it is you want. Most people never do that. Second, determine the price you're going to have to pay to get it, and
then resolve to pay that price.
—H.L. Hunt, oil billionaire (quoted in *Maximum Achievement*, 141)

I had decided once and for all, I was going to make it or die.
—John H. Johnson, founder of *Ebony* Magazine (quoted in Gross, 147)

Successful people are successful because they decide to be successful. Yes, they may have been born smart, rich, beautiful, but they still had to decide to take advantage of their good fortune. A vision without a decision to achieve it is a worthless pipedream. Vision in the absence of a decision is customarily evidenced by an excuse why the vision cannot be achieved. This behavior is usually indulged in by the lazy, the inept, those who never did and never will, and those whose mantra is "would have, could have, and should have," the regret that fuels their despair. Don't join them.

We can only recognize things for which we already have a mental map. A decision to achieve your goal creates a mental map for success in that endeavor. Creation of the mental map for success in an endeavor allows you to see pertinent opportunities that would have previously gone unnoticed, opening a door to an entire world you didn't even know existed. You begin to see opportunity everywhere you go because you are looking for opportunity. A critic always sees something to criticize. That is what they are looking for, so that is what they see. Once you decide to be successful, opportunity is what you will be looking for, so opportunity is what you will see.

There is a significant difference between a desire for success and a decision for success. Desire precedes decision. Decision precedes results. Desire, by itself, changes nothing, but a decision changes everything all by itself. Most people desire success; few decide to be a success. Whiners desire; winners decide.

If you listen to a person's language, they will tell you whether they are whiners or winners with respect to a given endeavor. Those who only desire success always have an excuse. They paint a pretty picture of their vision and then complain about how unfair things are, or talk about what they would do, but blah, blah, blah. A winner decides to be successful and then pays the cost, regardless of price. The difference between those who bask in the glow of success and those who wallow in mediocrity is rarely talent. In most cases, the difference is a decision to pay the price. Whiners waste time complaining about how things should be, but winners decide to pay the price, whatever it may be.

Champions are made when their skills are perfected in relative obscurity and without fanfare.
—Christopher I. Franklin

The Power of Decision

You can be what you will be.
—George S. Patton (quoted in D'Este, 87)

A ship in port is safe, but that's not what ships are for.
—Grace Hopper (quoted in *Profiles of Female Genius*, 34)

A decision allows you to be a victor and not a victim; to be proactive instead of reactive; to control your future and not be controlled by the fickle winds of fate and the ravaging winds of emotion. Once you've made a decision, it won't matter how you feel, what happens, what doesn't happen, or what others do. You will make your imprint on your surroundings, instead of being at the mercy of whatever happens to you.

Most people who fail to live their dreams fail because they spend more time worrying about what others may think than deciding what they want for themselves. A decision is a suit of armor that will protect you from the rocks and arrows that others will inevitably sling. A suit that will allow you to keep going whether others help you, hurt you, criticize you, or ridicule you out of lack of vision or love.

A decision is more powerful than fear. A mother whose child is in danger will be more moved by the decision to save her child than by the danger. A hero is not just a sandwich, nor is a hero a hero because of the absence of fear. A hero is a hero because he/she decided to move in spite of fear.

A decision gives courage, allowing you to let go of the familiar but unsatisfying old, and reach for the new. No matter how great the vision, without a decision to reach the brass ring, nothing changes. Dreamers dream dreams. Decision-makers make dreams come true.

A decision to succeed allows you to have a positive attitude. Once you have assessed your current situation, if you find yourself in a hole, a positive mental attitude allows you to say, "Great. The deeper the hole, the stronger the foundation," and then get to work laying bricks.

A decision propels you through previous personal boundaries. Most boundaries are internal but are manifested in external circumstances. A decision is the key to changing external circumstances and breaking through to new levels of rewards.

A decision allows you to operate economically. It enables you move forward without wasting effort on issues not directly germane to your goal.

Until you make the decision to leave the port of your discontent, you will never see the rewards of success. The struggles on the journey of success may be hard, but they are temporary. Quitting and failure take a lifetime, and the regrets are forever.

A decision that you want is much different from a decision that you will. A decision that you want is a wish; a decision that you will is power.

Willpower is a decision from which you do not retreat.

Persistence is a decision made over and over again.

Nothing in the world can take the place of persistence. Talent will not; nothing is more common than unsuccessful men with talent. Genius will not; unrewarded genius is almost a proverb. Education will not; the world is full of educated derelicts. Persistence and determination alone are omnipotent.

—Calvin Coolidge (quoted in *Live Your Dreams*, 39)

Successful People are Intentional

Successful people begin with the end result in mind. Intent requires a decision. A great example of what it is to be intentional is your attitude when you have decided to get to your warm comfortable home on a cold winter evening. If you get to the bus stop just as the bus pulls off, you don't decide to sleep on the street. You either wait for the next bus or find another way home. Treat every goal you decide to achieve as home. Anything in your past that interferes with your path home is simply a missed bus. Treat it like any other missed bus. Either wait for the next one or find another way home. Anything in your present that blocks your path is simply a detour sign. Treat it like any other detour. Find another way home.

In success, as in life, you are prepared for the detour if you are definite in your goals but flexible on the path. Anything in your path that slows you down is simply traffic. You are prepared for traffic if you are committed to your destination.

If you miss an opportunity, don't quit. Quitting would be analogous to sleeping on the street because you missed the bus. Prepare, as you wait for the next opportunity or search for another way to reach your goal. If some decision in your past prevents you from achieving your goal, don't simply take no for an answer and quit. Find another path.

If you don't have what you need in your possession to get what you want, don't quit. Break down your ultimate goal into smaller goals or steps. The next step or rung is to get what you need so that you can get what you want. If it is taking longer to achieve your goal than you would like, don't quit. You are simply in traffic. Stay committed to your commitment, and you will succeed. Quitters find a reason to quit; successful people find a reason to succeed. Nothing can stop a man or woman who has decided to not quit.

No Action Means There Was No Decision

The mind is its own place, and in itself can make heav'n of hell, and hell of heav'n.
—John Milton, *Paradise Lost*

Every decision to reach a goal or change a circumstance must result in an action. If there is no action, there was no real decision. Every decision must move you toward your goal, toward which all movement is ultimately directed, and measured against. Anyone can respond to an impulse to start up the mountain, but it takes a decision to compel you to keep going when you no longer feel like it. A decision enables you to remain fixed in the face of opposition and ridicule. At their core, what are often referred to as discipline, determination, resolution, commitment, and/or courage are simply decisions made in spite of, and over and over again.

Even no decision is a decision. It is a decision to remain where you are, which is what most people do. Then they complain about the same thing repeatedly, but always have an excuse why they cannot do anything to change their circumstances. They have made a decision to become comfortable in their discomfort.

Once you have created a vision of your destination and have made a decision to reach your goal, your greatest potential ally, and enemy, is in your own mind. Avoid deluding yourself and take the following affirmative steps to create an environment that supports your decision to be successful:

1. *Discipline Your Lifestyle*
   Develop systems and routines, especially in areas crucial to your long-term growth and success. Consistent growth is like compound interest. Rome wasn't built in a day, but it was built daily.

2. *Discipline Your Thinking*
   The Bible says, "As a man thinketh, so he is." In other words, you are what you think, and what you think is your reality. Exercising control over what you think will inevitably result in more control over what you say, do, and receive. Release anything that impedes your progress. Leave the excess baggage from your past behind—the wrong relationships, the mistakes, the gaffes, the regrets, the anger, and the animosity. You become what you think, so if you want to change your life, change your thinking. Train your thinking by feeding it what you desire to become, not what you desire to leave behind.

Determine Where You Are

In order to create a plan to fulfill your vision and reach your goal, you must determine where you are. Honestly assess your current reality without becoming emotionally incapacitated by it. An honest assessment will allow you to determine the steps, tools, processes, and changes necessary to make tomorrow's vision a reality. It will also allow you to determine the supporting structures necessary for you to make daily progress toward your desired end result.

A complete assessment must include who you are, where you are, what you do, who is around you, and the impact of each on your ability to achieve your goal. A decision to be a success allows you to allow others to be honest with you. When you have decided to be successful, you don't allow your feelings or ego to control the receipt of information that will aid in the achievement of your goals.

Pilots Have Flight Plans, So Should You

I didn't waste thirty-five years. I wasted a second, then a minute, then an hour, then a day, and the days grew into weeks, and here I am. It happened gradually, and one day I looked around and all those years had passed me by.
(Excerpted from *It's Not Over until You Win*, 232)

With your vision firmly in mind, and your decision made, the next step is to put together a plan, a road map of how to reach your goal. Many people look back at their lives and wonder how they ended up where they are. Many got there by not working their plan. Some never even had a plan.

Not working your plan in life is like getting on a series of buses, planes, trains, and automobiles while wearing a blindfold, getting on whatever happens to come along. The odds of you ending up in front of your house are not in your favor. Remember, when the odds are not in your favor, either find another route, or don't play. Yet this is the way many people live their lives.

Few people would intentionally get on a plane flown by a captain without a flight plan and a specific destination in mind. There is no telling exactly where the plane would land, but it probably won't be somewhere that everybody on board wants to go. You are the captain of your ship. Without a plan, your life may not end up exactly where you want it to go.

It is axiomatic that the more time you spend planning on the front end, the less time you will spend regretting on the tail end. You probably know someone who routinely ignores the instructions while attempting to put together or operate a new product. After they just can't seem to make it work properly or utilize the product to its full potential, they finally read the instructions; some people never do. Don't treat your life that way. Time is a truly scarce resource that you cannot replace. Don't waste your time flying around without a plan. To waste your time is to waste your life.

Be Definite on the Goal, but Flexible on the Path

If you are broke and someone writes you a large check, you will probably be determined to get to the bank to cash it. If you don't know where the bank is, you will look it up, or you will ask someone. If you ask someone for directions or for a ride and they can't or won't help you, you won't stop looking for the bank, nor are you likely to become any less determined to find it.

Similarly, if you are working toward fulfilling your dream, whether selling a product or pursuing an idea, and someone doesn't see the value in what you are sharing with them, it makes no sense to become discouraged or to quit then either. To become disillusioned or to quit because somebody else couldn't or wouldn't help you with your vision is akin to handing your future over to somebody else. Handing over your future and that of your family to someone who neither knows what you know nor can see what you see is foolish. Simply view that interaction as a path that didn't work.

If you are looking for a way across town and drive into a beautiful cul-de-sac, it may be beautiful, but it is still a cul-de-sac. You don't sit there and complain about it being a cul-de-sac, you turn around and find a through street. Similarly, maybe you made a presentation to, or had an interview with, just the right person. If they get it, if they see the value and they give you the job, life changes, and you are on your way. Great! If they don't get it, don't sit there and whine. Turn around and look for a through street. Be definite about the goal but flexible about the path to achieve it.

Success is a Process

> *Everybody applauds the successes, but what is*
> *missed in the midst of the cheering is that success*
> *is the end result of going through a process.*
> —Christopher I. Franklin

Question: How do you eat an elephant?
Answer: One bite at a time.

The joke is very old, but the point is valid.

1. *Break the Task Down*

   You've heard that Rome wasn't built in a day, and
   that a journey of a thousand miles begins with the
   first step. Since familiarity tends to breed contempt,
   these aphorisms may seem trite or mere clichés,
   but take care not to miss the point. In short, success is a process, not an event. Once you've identified your goal, grasping this point allows you to
   break the goal down into a series of manageable
   steps. Deciding to read five pages a day is much
   more manageable, and a commitment much more
   likely to be fulfilled, than simply saying, "One day
   I'm going to read *War and Peace.*"

   Breaking your goal down into manageable
   steps allows you to become systematic in your approach. Following a system allows you to make
   progress, regardless of how you feel, and provides easy benchmarks for determining progress.
   Either you read five pages today, or you didn't.

You are either going to get out of bed and read them now, or you're not. Failing to break your goal down into manageable steps dooms your goal to the abyss of good intentions. Good intentions are worthless in the absence of a decision resulting in action.

2. *Prepare, Prepare, Prepare*
The Boy Scouts have it right—be prepared. Investor Warren Buffett says it this way: "If you want to shoot rare, fast-moving elephants, you should always carry a loaded gun" (quoted in O'Loughlin, 194). If you've done it a thousand times already, you know that you can do it, and are less likely to freeze at the crucial moment. If you've put in the time to study the material and have not crammed at the last minute, you will be comfortable answering questions. In fact you will look forward to answering questions. Preparation is the key that frees us to enjoy our moment in the sun. When you've done a good job, you can't wait to turn your project in. When you've pushed through the excuses, and pushed away from the table, you can't wait to put on that outfit.

3. *Take Action*
In the end, it won't matter that you attended all the lectures, did all the analysis, understood all the theories, or that you've read this book or any other book, unless you take action. Action is the bridge between dreaming and achieving. To go

from being a dreamer to being an achiever, you must first become a doer. The heaviest weight is deadweight. It takes more power to get the train moving than to keep it moving.

Dreaming without moving is useless. The value of any dream is determined by the movement that follows; the value of inspiration is determined by the amount of perspiration that follows. Life rewards movement. To move from being among the many who talk the walk to the few who walk the talk, you must become a doer. To achieve greatness in any arena of your life, spiritual, personal, or business, you must take action.

Parties who want milk should not seat themselves on a stool in the middle of the field and hope that the cow will back up to them.
—Albert Hubert (quoted in *17 Essential Qualities of a Team Player,* 59)

Falling is Part of the Process

I never let my mistakes defeat or distract me, but I learn from them and move forward in a positive way.
—Lillian Vernon (quoted in *Profiles of Female Genius,* 348)

When you fall short of achieving your goal, it is often called *failing.* Maybe you didn't get the client, didn't pass the class, or didn't close the deal. Losers see failing as final, but failing isn't final unless you fail to get up. Success is a process that you cannot talk out; you must walk it out. Every baby falls while learning to walk. Winners understand that failing is as much a part of the process of success as falling is part of the process of learning to walk. Winners see failure as a guide helping to identify the right paths to their destination. They take the lessons from failure, use them to better prepare, then go right out and put what they have learned to work.

Winners see losing as an external event. Losers see it as an internal condition. Winners fail more than losers, because they keep asking and reaching for their goals long after losers have quit trying. Winners fail faster than losers because, while the loser is wallowing in self-pity over an unopened door, the winner has knocked on several doors. Because winners have decided that success is the only option, they doggedly continue toward the goal. Their decision to succeed allows every fall to serve as a stepping-stone, a lamp that illuminates their path to the top.

> *Once you embrace unpleasant news not as negative but as evidence of a need for change, you aren't defeated by it. You're learning from it.*
> —Bill Gates (quoted in Manz, 17)

Build Your Winner's Circle

Of his disciples . . . Jesus ordained twelve that they should be with Him.
—Mark 3:7-14

We should not only use all the brains we have, but all that we can borrow.
—Woodrow Wilson (quoted in *The Journey from Success to Significance*, 90)

The people in your life should be there by choice, not by chance. The energy and enthusiasm emanating from the winner's circle at the end of an event is almost palpable. This is where you will find the men and women who have been with the champion through the ups and downs, the years and the tears leading to this moment. It is in the winner's circle that you will find the core of a team whose whole is worth more than the sum of its parts. It is in the winner's circle that you will find those who understand that five fingers moving in unison are much more powerful than the same five fingers separate and apart.

The heavyweight boxing champion does not become the champion by relying on whoever happens to drop by his corner on fight night. The professional racecar driver does not become the champion by relying on a pit crew made up of whoever happens to be around on race day.

Champions do not stake their life goals on whoever happens to be around. And neither should you. Be intentional about the people in your life. Every relationship either adds to your life or takes away from your life. Every relationship either helps you stay between the lines as you travel life's highways, or nudges you off course.

Building a team takes patience and planning. Over time, you will find that you need different teams for different endeavors, but no matter what type of team you are building, whether it is your first team or your last team, the most important thing is to recruit the right people. Your team should be unified in its vision, but diversified in its skills.

Because you attract what you are, not what you want, as you improve, your team will improve. If you are always the smartest person on the team on every subject, the makeup of your team is flawed, and the team is unlikely to achieve greatness. In building your team, as in achieving your goal, you should be determined about the goal but flexible about the path.

Your winner's circle needs someone who will tell you when you're right, tell you when you're wrong, lift you up when you're weak, and keep you humble when you're strong. Someone who will cry with you in your moments of sorrow, but remind you of your bright tomorrows. Every winner's circle needs a friend. "As iron sharpens iron, friends sharpen the minds of each other" (Proverbs 27:17).

Do not confuse a friend with a yes-man. A yes-man on the inside will do far more damage than a known enemy on the outside. A yes-man cannot help you grow. Nor can he serve as a legitimate sounding-board for your ideas. A yes-man in your winner's circle is akin to believing your own press clippings. Add a yes-man to your team at your peril.

Do add to your winner's circle a solid supporter and friend. Seek for your winner's circle people who will help you to improve and/or advance toward your goals. People who are able, willing, and ready to lift up others are invaluable, and will have an exponential effect on your ability to get things done.

There is no magic number of people needed for your winner's circle. In fact, you and one can do plenty. The Green Hornet had Kato; Batman had Robin (and Batgirl); Bruce Wayne had Dick Grayson, Clark Kent had Lois Lane (and Jimmy Olsen); Superman had the Super Friends; Captain had Tennille; Wilma had Betty; Thelma had Louise; Bonnie had Clyde; Tom had Jerry; and Mutt had Jeff. Heck, even the Lone Ranger had Tonto!!!

Who is going to be your sidekick, your right-hand man, your faithful companion, your comrade-in-arms, your soul mate, your road dog? Build yourself a winner's circle. If Don Quixote could find someone to go with him to chase windmills, certainly you can find someone to take with you on your journey to the top.

Of the 12, Jesus chose Peter, James and John.

Some people should be kept closer than others.

THE FRANKLIN KEYS TO UNLIMITED POSSIBILITIES

4. Make a Decision

Successful people are successful because they decide to be successful. A vision without a decision to achieve it is worthless, and is customarily evidenced by an excuse why the vision cannot be achieved. Every decision must result in an action. If there is no action toward change, there was no decision to change. With your vision centered and your decision made, the next step is to put together a plan, a road map of how to reach your goal. You must be definite about the goal, but flexible about the path to achieve it.

FRANKLIN KEY NUMBER 5: <u>SACRIFICE</u>

If you don't get what you want, it is a sign that you did not seriously want it, or that you tried to bargain over the price.
—Rudyard Kipling (quoted in *The Journey from Success to Significance*, 51)

The Road to Success is a Toll Road

Greatness results from self-leadership. Self-leadership results from self-discipline. Self-discipline results from consistently repeated sacrifice. Greatness, leadership, achievement, and success always require sacrifice. Great leadership, great achievement, and great success always require great sacrifice. Sacrifice is the price of success in any endeavor. To have success, you must be willing to sacrifice to reach the goal. Whether the price is high or low, the price must be paid before the goal can be achieved. No matter how loudly or how often you proclaim your desire for success, the true indicator of how much you want success is determined by the amount you are willing to sacrifice to achieve it. Your willingness to sacrifice will always be the determining factor in whether or not you are successful in achieving your goals. You will only be willing to sacrifice to the extent that the value of your vision is clear. The value of your vision can only be clear if you are clear on the vision itself. There will always be a direct correlation between the amount you are willing to sacrifice and the clarity of your vision. The clearer you are about your desired end result, aka your vision, the more you will be willing to sacrifice to make it a reality.

In the dictionary, as in life, you will find *sacrifice* before you find *success*. You cannot reap before you sow. You must plant a seed for a tree to grow. Your sacrifice today is the seed of your success tomorrow. The philosopher Nietzsche said that when your *why* is strong enough, you can bear any *how*.

In other words, if your vision is strong enough, if the value you place on success is high enough, any sacrifice will seem a small price to pay. Your "why" is what gets you up in the morning. It can't be the money, because money in itself has no value. You can't eat it, you can't wear it, and you'd have to burn it in order for it to keep you warm.

But your "why" can be what you can do with the money. Send your kids to better schools, quit the job that you only go to because you have bills, buy that beach house are all things that you can do with the money. They can serve as a reason why you are willing to do what you are willing to do. The "how" that you bear is the sacrifice you must pay today in order to make your vision your reality. If your vision of success is strong enough, you can pay any price.

Jesus endured the cross because he had a vision of re-joining his Father after having reconciled us to God. His internal vision of the future was so bright that it allowed Him to withstand the painful present. Martin Luther King had a dream. His dream allowed him to say that "longevity has its place," but if he had to go he didn't mind. You see, he too had a vision.

How much do you really value your vision? Would you sacrifice twenty minutes of your favorite television show each night? In the absence of vision, some will ask, "Why should I?" Would you sacrifice twenty minutes of your favorite television show in exchange for your life or the life of your child or significant other? Would you give up twenty minutes of a football game so that an elderly family member could retire? Would you sacrifice twenty minutes each night so that you could take those you love on a vacation every year and not have to worry about the financial cost? In exchange for a life, or for living your desired lifestyle, twenty minutes would seem to be a small price to pay.

Would you spend six months digging a poorly ventilated tunnel with poorly made tools in exchange for $1 per hour? Not likely! Would you spend six months digging a poorly ventilated tunnel with poorly made tools in exchange for your freedom? More likely than not!! If you could "see" the future, would you give $1 today in exchange for $10 tomorrow? Maybe you would. Would you invest $100 today for a return of $1,000,000 tomorrow? Of course you would! Vision creates value. If the value of your vision is high enough, any sacrifice will seem a small price to pay.

In its highest form, when you are running your own race in business and in life, sacrifice won't feel like sacrifice, and work won't seem like work. When you love what you do, you will find yourself like an athlete or musician in the "zone," where your work is pure fun. But no matter how much you pay for success, failure always costs more. The price of failure is regret. Nothing costs or weighs more than regret.

> *Choose work you love, and you will never have to work a day in your life.*
> —Confucius (quoted in Shula and Blanchard, 69)

Paying the Price for Relationships

True greatness can only be achieved through relationships with others. And every relationship either adds to your life or takes away from it. There is a price you pay when you are not intentional in choosing your relationships. But there is also a price to pay when you are intentional about your relationships. Being intentional about your relationship may require you to weed out friends, business associates, and perhaps even some family members who are counterproductive to your dream. It won't always feel good, but it may be required. The price you pay is the sacrifice you make for reaching your dream.

Examine the people you choose to spend most of your time with. Some relationships may be good to you, but may not be good *for* you. Wrong relationships in your life can prevent your ship from ever leaving the shore of discontent and derail your train far before it reaches the station. If two pianos are sitting side by side, the note played on one piano will vibrate on the other. What you see in the lives of the people you choose to spend most of your time with will echo in your life.

If six grandfather clocks are standing side by side, their pendulums swinging at different intervals, within a short period all of the pendulums will be swinging in sync. Scientists call this phenomenon *entrainment.* Older generations didn't speak of entrainment; they simply said, If you lie down with dogs, you will get up with fleas. Whatever you call it, do not get in sync with people who are not going where you want to go. Unless the people around you are helping you move toward your goal, they are moving you away from it. It is imperative that you avoid relationships that bring you down.

Seek out relationships that build you up. Get in sync with people who are walking your path, or who have already walked your path. Be intentional about who you spend your time with.

All great athletes have at least one coach. Find yourself a coach, a mentor, someone who can help you navigate the challenges on your path to greatness. It does not have to be someone you know. Go to the library, the bookstore, and read the books, and listen to the tapes of those who have walked the path you dream of walking. Follow the trail they have blazed, until you can blaze trails of your own, and then leave a trail for others to follow.

After becoming intentional about your relationships, you must strive to become a resource to the people in your relationships. When you become a resource to the people in your relationships, the people in your relationships will become an incredible resource to you. Approach your relationships in terms of what you can give, instead of what you can get. Business philosopher Jim Rohn's mantra is that if you help enough people get what they want, you will get everything you want.

The advantages that will result from focusing on what you can give instead of what you can gain will, over time, provide benefits far superior to the short-term gains that may result from selfishness. As a businessperson, if you focus on what you can give instead of what you can get, your customers will see you as a resource. This will give you an advantage over your competitors who your customers view solely as salespersons.

As a leader, your ability to influence and develop mutually beneficial relationships with others will be based upon their perception of your value. Their perception of your value will be primarily based upon your ability to listen, learn, and endeavor to meet the needs, wants, and desires of those around you. For leaders, taking care of business means taking care of results and relationships. Businesses fail because of bad results, and succeed because of good results.

But good relationships are more than something nice to have. Good relationships provide the business advantage that is the catalyst for good results. Your skills matter, but many businesses and lives have failed where the owner had great skills. Would you consistently eat in an expensive restaurant where you didn't feel welcome? Or would you prefer an expensive restaurant where everybody makes you feel welcome? Is the twelfth man on a basketball team usually so much better than everybody else that didn't make the team? Relationships and results matter.

As a leader, competence in your craft should be a given. You may be the world's best accountant, but few people can tell the difference in skills among accountants. You may be a world-class market analyst, but the information available to you is generally the same information available to your competition. So even if you are the world's best market analyst or accountant, your talent will not guarantee you success.

In fact, whether you even get an opportunity to showcase your skills will often be dependent upon the strength of your relationships. As an employee, employer, business owner, or entrepreneur, your skills matter, but your relationships will be the determining factor in your success. Great skills and bad relationships may get you by in the short term, but not in the long term. In the long term, great skills and great relationships will always succeed.

Focus on and invest in the maintenance and growth of your personal relationships and your business relationships. Do not make the mistake of thinking you can mistreat some relationships without infecting the others. You cannot mistreat teammates, employees, vendors, or your personal relationships without infecting your customer relationships. Everybody has customers, and an infectious attitude infects all it comes in contact with.

As an employer, how you treat your employees is how they will treat your customers. If you do not focus on the needs of your employees when you speak to them, your employees will not focus on the needs of your customers when they speak to them. If you fail to control your emotions when speaking to your family, when it matters most, you will fail to control your emotions when speaking to your customers.

As an employee, until you learn how to treat your employer's time and equipment with care, you will not learn how to treat your own time and equipment with care. If you are an employee without external customers, your boss, subordinates, or other coworkers are your internal customers. As a would-be entrepreneur, the sooner you decide to care for your employer's customers, the sooner you will be prepared to care for customers of your own.

The more consistently intentional you are about your relationships, the more quickly you will create an environment conducive to your success. Part of creating an environment conducive to success requires that you always do your best. Sometimes we choose to be less than our best because we want to fit in, or don't want our friends or somebody else to feel bad. Run—do not walk—from any relationship that requires you to do less than your best in order to fit in. If you choose to do less than your best for the sake of your friends, you need new friends, and you are sabotaging your own success.

Doing less than your best to fit in is selfish, self-serving, self-destructive, egotistical, and does a disservice to your friend. It is selfish because it shows that you are more interested in having "peace" with this person than you are in helping them to be the best they can be. Self-serving and self-destructive, because you are choosing to intentionally debase yourself so that you can be liked. It is egotistical because it is based upon a belief that you are so great, that your light is so bright, that your friend cannot handle it. As Nelson Mandela said, "There is nothing enlightened about shrinking so that others won't feel insecure around us. . . . And as we let our own light shine, we unconsciously give other people permission to do the same" (Thomas, 13-14).

Open Your Ears More Than Your Mouth

*I remind myself every morning: Nothing I say this
day will teach me anything. So if I'm going to
learn, I must do it by listening.*
—Larry King

None of us is as smart as all of us.
—Japanese proverb (quoted in Goleman, 198)

Beware of the disease that seems to infect many leaders as they move up the ladder. It seems that the higher
they go, the bigger their mouths grow, and the smaller
their ears become. This disease is dumb, wasteful, and
dangerous. It cuts leaders off from the foundation of
their success, the "little people" closer to the ground, so
they never hear the warnings of change coming until
it's too late, and undermines everything that has been
done up to this point, wasting all the valuable time they
spent intentionally seeking, recruiting, and developing
their greatest resource—great people.

As a leader, it is foolish to assemble a great team and
then treat the members as serfs whose role is to simply
do your bidding. If you do, you won't have great talent
on your team very long and will miss out on the benefits.

When people believe what they say to you doesn't
matter, they won't bother to say much. So the next time
you see an executive perched on a ladder resting on a
shaky foundation, oblivious to the winds that everybody
in the street knows are blowing, and losing the few good
people left in the company, you know what the final

analysis will show: His mouth got bigger, and his ears got smaller, and then Humpty went tumbling down.

Good leadership and good relationships require good communication. Good communication begins with good listening. Good leaders listen. Good friends listen. Good parents listen. Good children listen. As a leader, it is imperative that you listen. Listen to your superiors, your subordinates. Listen to people you are smarter than, and people who are smarter than you. You can learn from all of them, even if it is only what not to do. The more you listen to people, the more people will listen to you. Listening fosters discussion; discussion foster creativity. Creativity fosters discovery; discovery fosters success.

Success, like creativity, is messy. It is filled with bumps, turn, detours, and uncharted terrain. As a leader, the available information that your decisions should ideally be based upon rarely shows up on your desk in one neat package. Instead, it often comes in disguise, in drips and drabs, and dispersed throughout your team. Creating an environment where people feel listened to and know that their opinions are valued gives you the best opportunity to get the information you need in time to make a difference. It will increase the flow of information within the team, stretch the envelope of your team's collective thinking, and result in increased team identity and effectiveness.

More often than not, the information that will allow a problem to be avoided, or that will lead to a breakthrough, is already somewhere in the organization. History is replete with examples: Eight months before the surprise dawn attack on Pearl Harbor a naval report concluded that a dawn attack on Pearl Harbor would achieve complete surprise.

Prior to the failure of the sealants that led to the explosion of the space shuttle Challenger, an engineer for the contractor urged his supervisor to delay the launch because the weather conditions could lead to the failure of the sealants. The subsequent investigation determined that the failed sealants were the cause of the disaster.

Xerox developed the computer that led to the groundbreaking success of Apple and Microsoft, but failed to exploit its own creation. Apple and Microsoft capitalized on Xerox's failure and created an entire industry.

A simple but crucial key to getting information in time to make a difference is *listening*.

As a leader, prior to making decisions, it is crucial that you consistently involve your team when trying to identify the best available options. You will maximize your ability to capitalize on your team's knowledge and experience if you refrain from starting discussions by stating your position. Failure to adhere to this rule will result in negative consequences that will not show up until time and money have been wasted. When you begin by stating your position, you potentially poison the well of creativity, since weak people may line up behind you because you are the leader, some telling you what they think you want to hear, others not telling you what they think you don't want to hear.

Even if your team is strong enough to avoid that issue, your opinion might still poison the well of creativity by limiting the framework of the debate. The information flow and perspectives that define the possible and the impossible, the dead end and the breakthrough, are all dependent upon the framework in which you are working. A limited framework limits the box from which your team will work. When you limit the box, or paradigm, from which your team works, you limit the flow of ideas and you limit your options. When you limit your options, you limit your ability to identify, and your flexibility to choose, the best paths to your goals.

Weak leaders avoid input from team members because they think that weakens their authority. Those who think this way fail to understand that debate is open for discussion, but decision-making is not; and that leadership makes you responsible, but not infallible.

President Woodrow Wilson said that we should not only use all the brains that we have, but all that we can borrow (*17 Indisputable Laws of Teamwork*, 7). Sam Walton, the creator of Wal-Mart, said he borrowed just about everything from someone else, and that he borrowed from the creator of Price Club more than anybody else (*Profiles of Genius*, 152). One of his rules of business was to listen to everyone in his company. If the President of the United States and one of the most successful businessmen of all times are willing to listen and borrow the ideas of others, shouldn't you do the same? But you won't be able to hear, much less borrow, many ideas if you are doing more talking than listening.

Strong leaders are intentional about involving their team in the success process by seeking out, and tapping into, their knowledge. Listening enables you to reap the benefits of the diversity of skills, perspectives, and experiences of your team members. A process in which ideas are generated, challenged, strengthened and/or discarded is invaluable before a decision is made. "I knew it" after the decision is implemented creates strife and adds no value.

Once a decision is made, debate stops. Everybody must get behind the decision, no matter what side of the debate they were on. When people are involved and feel free to state their opinion before a decision is made, they feel comfortable buying in to the end result after a decision is made. When people buy in to the end result, it is much easier for them emotionally to support its implementation.

As a leader if you are intentional about creating this type of environment, you will reap benefits unattainable by weaker leaders. If you spend more time asking, rather than telling your team, you will spend more time leading, rather than following, your competitors in the marketplace.

Involved, creative people seeking the best path on the murky road to success will often have conflicting views on the best way to get there. But properly focused conflict is not part of the problem; it is part of the solution. It is the crucible of conflict that provides the objective assessments, divergent perspectives, and potential courses of action necessary for informed decision-making. This is why it is important that team members feel free to attack each other's ideas but never each other. Properly focused conflict is the catalyst for creativity, and the furnace for separating the bad ideas from the good ideas, and the merely good ideas from the best ideas. It increases the flow of information across the organization; focuses thinking; identifies potential problems and potential opportunities; curtails groupthink; reinforces excellence as the organization's cultural standard; and increases commitment to implementation of the final decision. The bad decisions avoided and the opportunities seized as a result of properly focused conflict will push your team far beyond anyplace it could have gone otherwise.

If as a leader you don't need input from team members because you are always the smartest person in the room on every subject, you need a new team. If you are not always the smartest person in the room on every subject, you need feedback. If you are sure you already know the answer, then seek confirmation by intentionally having your ideas challenged. Having your ideas challenged will serve as a safeguard against the human tendency of falling in love with our own ideas. If you are right, then your greatness has been confirmed again. If you are wrong, in total or in part, listening will allow you to move ahead by learning and correcting errors in private, rather than wasting resources and being proven wrong in public.

When you listen to others, listen actively. Focus on the speaker. Imagine how focused you would be if the person speaking to you was someone you always wanted to meet. Give that same intensity of focus, no matter who is speaking to you. Look the speaker in the eye. Resist the urge to look around the room or become otherwise distracted by whatever else is going on around you.

101

Don't simply wait to respond. It is difficult to listen when you are planning what to say. Be sensitive to the speaker's words, body language, and the emotional context. Paraphrase, probe, ask leading questions, and extend their argument. Determine if the person is finished speaking, then reflect before you respond. A pause of only a few seconds will add substance to what you say and to the hearer's perception of what you say. These simple steps will make the person you are speaking with feel important; they will feel respected; they will feel that they have been heard; and they will feel that you care. Even if they don't get what they want, they will feel that you listened.

Listen, listen, listen to the people who do the work.
—H. Ross Perot (quoted in Waterman, 136)

Schedule Your Priorities

*Things which matter most should never be at the
mercy of things which matter least.*
—Goethe (quoted in Cooper, 110)

To prioritize is to do what you must do now in the
short term so that in the long term you can do whatever
you want to do. Above-average people prioritize their
schedule. Leaders schedule their priorities. The difference is significant. Most of you put your most pressing
matters on your schedule, so it follows that when you
prioritize your schedule, what's most pressing is what will
get done. The problem with this is that what is most pressing in the short term is often not the same as what is most
important in the long term. Consequently, what is most
pressing often gets done at the expense of what is
most important. When this happens, it can feel as
though the harder you work, the farther you fall behind.
This is not far from the truth. What really happens is
that you fall farther behind in important matters. The
way to avoid this trap is to schedule your priorities. When
you schedule your priorities, what is most important always gets done in its proper order. You stay on target toward your most important goals, and you do first things
first until the first thing is done.

Sometimes it can be difficult to distinguish what is
most pressing from what is most important. In fact, the
mistake of selecting what's most pressing at the expense
of what's most important is easy to make and happens
often. For example, Morgan has a rough day and de-

cides to buy a new outfit to cheer herself up, so she makes a mental note to go by the mall on her way home. Leaving the office behind, she takes a breath, thinks of how much she hates her job and has to get her business started as soon as possible. She can't wait to leave her stressful boss behind. She gets to the mall and finds a great outfit. It costs a little more than she wanted to spend, but she knows where to find the perfect shoes that match. She buys the outfit, picks up the shoes, and heads home feeling much better.

The extra money she spent was supposed to go into her retirement account, which she plans to use to fund her business. Probably without even realizing it, Morgan just pushed her ability to leave her job behind a little farther away. Putting money into her retirement account was more important than buying the outfit, but her desire for the outfit was more pressing. What's most pressing always clamors for attention and can easily obscure what's most important. Scheduling our priorities helps avoid this trap.

If Morgan had scheduled her priorities, her retirement fund money would have been put aside first. Then she would have looked at her options and determined the best way to treat herself to a new outfit. She would have met her short-term needs without compromising her long-term goal of having enough money to start her own business as soon as possible. Morgan made the common mistake of doing what was most pressing at the expense of what was most important.

You may not be a "shopper" like Morgan, but we often

succumb to the same pressures. Though it may take on a different form, the results are the same. We need to work out, but we choose to sleep in. We need to eat better, but we choose to go through the drive-thru. The kids need to read more, but we choose to let them watch TV. All these may appear mere trifles, until 20 lbs later and the bad cholesterol is off the charts, and the kids are having problems in school. Scheduling your priorities helps to keep mere trifles from becoming major crises.

In the workplace it is easy to spend an entire day putting out one fire after another and at the end of the day feel like you've accomplished nothing at all. That intuitive sense of failure, or where-did-the-day-go bewilderment, can be disconcerting after being busy all day. This disconcerting feeling arises because despite their demand for attention, most "fires" we spend the day handling are most pressing and are done at the expense of what is most important.

Contrast that disconcerting feeling with the sense of accomplishment you feel after spending an entire day working on and completing your most important project. Your message light is blinking, your email inbox looks like you've been out of the office, and you're leaving the office late, but you feel great. Why? Because that feeling, that sense of accomplishment, is what comes from doing what is most important.

The sense of failure comes from doing what is most pressing. Admittedly the distinction can be unclear. But it becomes even easier to miss if you have not scheduled your priorities in advance. When you don't schedule your priorities in advance, you don't have a context in which to evaluate the matters demanding your attention.

Leaders plan their day. An effectively planned day has priorities scheduled. Scheduled priorities give the day focus and context. This is important because the best use of your time is to always work on the most important thing until you can't work on it anymore. Then you move on to the next most important thing. If you plan your day, when pressing issues begin to noisily demand your attention, you have a context in which to evaluate them. If the new issue does *not* support your scheduled priorities, the question is, Does it have a higher priority? If the new issue *does* support your scheduled priorities, the question is, Does it have a higher priority than that portion of the project you are currently working on? If the issue demanding your attention is not new, you already determined it was less important than your scheduled priorities when you planned your day.

Even if you do have to change your plans, you will benefit from having had a plan to begin with. You will have momentum and focus going into the change, and you will know where to pick up when the reason for the change is over.

Because leaders play multiple roles in life, often with conflicting demands, unless priorities are clearly thought out and identified, it is easy to find your ability to function, or even to think clearly, overwhelmed. When someone says that they have so much to do that they don't know where to start, what they are really saying is, they haven't prioritized and they don't have a plan.

If you do not have a plan for your life or for your day, or if you have a plan but have not scheduled your priorities to make the plan a reality, you may be working hard, but you are not working smart. "Work hard and grow rich" is not the title of a classic book, nor is it sage advice that you are likely to hear from successful people. You may hear someone say, "Work hard and get good grades," or "Work hard to feed your family," but you will not often hear, "Work hard and grow rich."

Riches are not for everybody. But if you want riches, however you define riches, it is not enough to simply work hard. Most of the hardest-working people in the world make the least amount of money and have few riches that most of us desire. The evidence of this is universal. So working hard in and of itself cannot be the answer.

Think and Grow Rich is the title of a classic book, and it is also very wise advice. The term should serve as a methodology that you can apply in your life and have immediate results. Think about and decide what you want to accomplish in your life or in your day. Once you have done this, you have defined what you will call success, the achievement of which will bring you riches, however you define it. You now have a goal on which to focus your energies. Then think about, identify, and prioritize the necessary steps to achieve your goal. You now have a map to where you want to go. These simple steps provide a context for you to evaluate your choices. The more consistently you align your choices with your map, and work on your highest priorities, the faster you will succeed.

Emergencies make their own schedules. If you have "routine emergencies" that happen every month, every quarter, every pay period, or some variation of the theme, they are not real emergencies. They are the results of poor planning and/or ineptitude. Outside of responding to emergencies, if you spend most of your day reacting instead of executing, you are not leading. You are simply blowing in the wind of whatever happens to come your way.

Success requires goals. Daily success requires daily goals. Daily goals without daily plans are merely daily wishes. Plan your life, and your day, by scheduling your priorities. Then work your plan. If you do, you will be well on your way to winning your own race in business and in life.

> *We are all pilgrims on the same journey . . . but some pilgrims have better road maps.*
> —Nelson DeMille

Risk: A Prerequisite of Greatness

Growth demands a temporary surrender of security.
—Gail Sheehy (quoted in *The Journey from Success to Significance*, 40)

The fishermen know that the sea is dangerous and the storm terrible, but they have never found these dangers sufficient reason for remaining ashore.
—Vincent Van Gogh

The word *risk* is often used as a euphemism for fear of loss. This misuse of the word protects the ego, at the cost of prohibiting progress. Society is so overwhelmingly fear-driven that things are called "risky" based on the perceived potential likelihood of the result we don't want, obscuring the true meaning of *risk*. Risk is a set of choices, the outcomes of which are not certain. To risk is to dare to choose. Success is the end result of persistently exercising choices that turn your dreams into your reality. All achievement comes down to choices. All choices contain elements of risk.

Leaders understand that to not choose is to choose, and that if they don't choose to control their destiny, they are choosing to have their destiny controlled by the choices of others. People will often say they elected to not do something because it was too risky. The statement is misleading. Most people will risk the price of a movie ticket where there is a 50/50 chance of a negative outcome. Most people will not risk their mortgage payment when there is a 50/50 chance of a negative outcome. Millions of people play lotteries even though the odds are at least a million to one against them winning. So it can't be the odds against winning that paralyzes most people.

What paralyzes most people is the fear of loss and/or the fear of failure. This causes a problem even in assessing the risk, because the focus is on the fear. Remember, we usually move in the direction of what we focus on the most. Who is most likely to succeed, the artist on the high wire looking at the ground, thinking about falling, or the one focused on getting to the other side? Greatness does not result from identifying problems. Greatness results from identifying and exploiting opportunities.

Failures and followers look for problems, and see problems. Leaders look for opportunities, and see opportunities. Failures and followers say the risk is too great to try. Leaders say the reward is too great not to try.

This does not mean that leaders are, or should be, reckless. They are not. Nor do they avoid risk at all cost. Leaders understand that the only thing promised is nothing, and that if they want more than nothing, they must make choices. All choices contain risks, so leaders know that they cannot avoid risk. They do, however, seek to control the amount of risk inherent in their choices.

Leaders are result-oriented and opportunity-focused. Their focus is on the outcome they want to create, so they create plans that fit the circumstances to exploit the opportunities. Because their plans are specifically created to match the circumstances, they are able to exert more influence over their risks than followers. Leaders also seek to minimize those areas of the outcome over which they cannot exert influence.

Followers are generally exposed to higher levels of risk than leaders. This is because followers make plans and then seek circumstances that fit their plans. The rigidity of this approach results in risks that are generally fixed, to the extent their plans and the circumstances do not perfectly match. Followers also pay a potentially more insidious price. Given the choice between a job that pays $7 an hour, and a job that pays $5.50 an hour plus commissions, most followers will take the job that pays the higher base salary. There is no risk that they will make more or less than $7 an hour. They have guaranteed themselves $7 an hour. They have also guaranteed themselves that they will have no opportunity to make more than $7 an hour, regardless of how much money they generate for the company, putting a hard cap on their income. Generally, the lower the risk level, the harder the cap on potential income.

The person who always complains about their dead-end job but never does anything to change their circumstances is making the same mistake as the person that took the job paying $7 an hour. Both may have big dreams, but they have no vision. They often talk about it, but they never seem able to "be about it." Instead of reaching for a destiny of their own choosing, they reach for security proffered by another. They never realized that the only thing job security does is lock away the ladder of success where you might be able to see it, but can never reach it.

> *They saw risk as a mere necessity in pursuing their goals.*
> —Gene Landrum (*Profiles of Female Genius*, 47)

Informed Risks: Not Wishful Thinking

> *A mountain is big or small not because of its height in the sky but because of what each person brings to the climb.*
> —(Cooper, 247)

The years of rehearsals, practices, tears, lessons learned, failures, and successes, the books read, and the seminars attended have provided teams and leaders with specialized knowledge and skills. This knowledge base and the team's organization competencies, coupled with the leader's positive attitude and adamant determination, are the foundation of the team's confidence. It is from this position of strength that leaders take risks. They do not take risk beyond the boundaries of these strengths.

Great leaders do not hesitate to make hard decisions or learn "new areas." But they do not take unnecessary risks in new areas until these new areas have become areas of expertise. Decisions are preceded by an objective analysis of all available information and team competencies.

In choosing to take the risk or sometimes even in assessing it, expertise may be brought in from outside organizations. Moms, mentors, lawyers, financial experts, and various consultants are often hired on a short-term basis to provide expertise that is not indigenous to the team. Entire business units may also be created or acquired to exploit an opportunity, depending on the price, fit, and expected return. Unnecessary risks are not undertaken based on wishful thinking or out of desperation. Leaders take informed risks based on personal and team competencies to exploit available opportunities.

> *I'm no genius, I'm smart in spots—but I stay around those spots.*
> —Thomas J. Watson, founder of IBM (quoted in O'Loughlin, 150)

Be Committed to Your Commitment

Successful people harness the power of commitment. Commitment is a decision evidenced by sustained action continued until completion. Absent action, an alleged commitment is at best an intention; at worst it's a lie made to oneself. Commitment separates losers from winners, cowards from the courageous, achievers from mere dreamers and be's from wannabes. Every successful person is a dreamer, but not every dreamer is a successful person. The difference between the two is commitment.

You are already committed to something. You are either committed to the cause and end of your choosing, or you are committed to reliance upon the unchanging uncertainties of life, the winds of chance, or the charity of others to determine your destiny. Only commitment to the end of your choosing will raise you to the greatness for which you were created. Any cause worthy of you requires commitment. Any cause that does not require your full commitment is, relatively speaking, a waste of your time. Author and speaker Tony Robbins says, "life's greatest rewards are reserved for those who demonstrate a never-ending commitment to act until they achieve" (Russell, 17). Harness the power of commitment.

Greatness is only achieved through commitment. Greatness must be a resolve, not simply an ambition. Only when you are resolved to greatness will you be committed to paying the price of greatness. Greatness is manifested under the bright lights where all can see, but it is created when few are watching. How many golf balls did Tiger Woods hit when there was no gallery? How many free throws did Michael Jordan shoot when there were no fans in the stands? How many songs did the Bee Gees sing when nobody was listening? How many speeches did Martin Luther King make in front of empty pews before he said, "I Have a Dream," in front of the world?

It has often been said that luck is when opportunity meets preparation. Commitment drives you to prepare when nobody is looking, so you can seize the opportunity when everybody is looking. Then those who don't understand the price you paid will say that you were lucky. But the truth is, you were prepared because you were committed. When you are committed to your commitment, "Ain't no mountain high enough, ain't no valley low enough, ain't no river wide enough"—Ashford & Simpson said it best—to keep you from living your dream.

Winners are persistent even in the absence of apparent progress. No matter how things may look, remember that the tortoise beat the hare and that the race is not always to the swift but to the one that keeps running. Persistence trumps resistance. A large rock thrown into a stream will temporarily displace the water, but in time the water will permanently change the rock.

Baseball player Cal Ripken won several Gold Glove Awards as a shortstop. However, his crowning achievement as a baseball player is the streak of consecutive games played. He was feted around the world for showing up more than anybody else. He was committed to his commitment.

1. *Commitment Begins with a Decision*
    Some people want everything to be perfect be-
    fore they're willing to commit themselves to any-
    thing. If you wait until all the lights are green
    before leaving home, you won't get very far. Com-
    mitment always precedes achievement.

2. *Commitment Is Evidenced by Sustained Action*
    Nothing is easier than talking the walk. Nothing
    is harder than walking the talk.

3. *Commitment Continues until Completion*
    Commitment is the enemy of resistance. The Bible
    states that the race is to him that keeps running.
    If you want to get anywhere worthwhile, you must
    be committed.

The secret of success is constancy to purpose.
—Benjamin Disraeli (quoted in *17 Essential Qualities
of a Team Player,* 89)

THE FRANKLIN KEYS TO UNLIMITED POSSIBILITIES

5. *Sacrifice*

Sacrifice is the price of success in any endeavor. The true indicator of how much you truly desire success is determined by the amount that you are willing to sacrifice to achieve it. You will only be willing to sacrifice to the extent that the value of your vision is clear. The clearer you are about your desired end result, aka your vision, the more you will be willing to sacrifice to make it a reality.

FRANKLIN KEY NUMBER 6: PERSONAL DEVELOPMENT IS THE DIFFERENCE BETWEEN POSSIBLE AND IMPOSSIBLE

Men are anxious to improve their circumstances, but are unwilling to improve themselves; they therefore remain bound.
—James Allen (*As a Man Thinketh*, 17)

It always seems impossible, until it's done.
—Nelson Mandela

Achieving a new vision requires a new level of accomplishment. A new level of accomplishment requires a new level of personal growth. Personal growth is internal change. Internal change is the catalyst for external change. Personal growth manifests itself in changes in behavior and in higher levels of accomplishment. We create internal change by changing what we read, what we listen to, who we associate with, what we think, and what we say.

An age-old aphorism states, when your only tool is a

hammer, you think that every problem is a nail. Your ability to recognize and seize opportunities, and to avoid potential problems, is directly related to the number of tools in your toolbox. The more tools at your disposal, the more you are able to see circumstances, situations, and opportunities from perspectives inaccessible to you when your only tool is a hammer.

You increase the number of tools in your toolbox through personal growth. Personal growth is the result of intentionally cultivating the mental, emotional, interpersonal, and character traits necessary for your success.

Success is the fruits of our lives. Personal growth is the root of our lives. The condition of the roots determines the condition of the fruits. If you want to improve the fruits of your life, you must improve the roots of your life.

Just as you have become intentional about your time, your relationships, and your future, you must become intentional about your personal growth. It is imperative that you develop a personal growth plan and be disciplined in adhering to that plan. Read the books, listen to the tapes, go to the presentations, use whatever methods of learning work best for you, but do something every day to make you better. Whether your plan calls for 20 minutes or one hour a day, it must be a daily discipline.

In the beginning, taking daily steps toward your goals is much more important than the size of the steps you take toward those goals. The most important thing is to keep stepping. When told of the need for a personal growth plan, too often the common cry is, "I don't have time." But unless you are experiencing your desired level of success, your circumstances show that you no longer have time *not* to follow a personal growth plan.

How we see any given set of facts is dependent upon the frame our minds place around those facts. Your ability to see opportunity where you at first saw defeat, and where others can only see defeat, is due to your ability to frame and reframe repeatedly until you see what you are looking for.

Experience enables us to see things we would not have been able to see years earlier. A personal growth plan allows us to harness and build on the experience of others without the years of mistakes that usually accompany years of experience.

If you want to improve your circumstances, you must first improve yourself.

A Rising Tide Lifts All Boats

Leaders are learners. As a rising tide lifts all boats, constantly learning is the tide upon which your organization will either rise or fall. Remember, you attract who you are, so when you are learning, you attract others who are learning, and your organization's tide is rising. If you continue to learn, you will continue to lead a rising organization. No matter how far down the leadership path you are, seek a mentor so that you can learn; and seek others to mentor so that they can learn. You do not have to join a formal mentoring program. But many churches, schools, and other civic organizations have such programs. There is always a need for mentors with your exact experience. Remember, seek to give as well as receive, and you will receive more than you expect.

Leaders are teachers. You can't teach what you don't know. And when you have taught all that you know, your organization will cease to grow. As a leader of leaders, your responsibility is to make other leaders better leaders. You cannot continue to make others better if you don't continue to get better.

It is not enough to hope your people learn by osmosis. You must be intentional about their development. Encourage them to attend the pertinent classes and seminars. The teamwork, camaraderie, and productivity that will result will more than compensate for the financial cost of the training. As a leader, one of your fundamental goals should be for the people who work with you to be better for having worked with you. Great leaders know that their organization can only be as good as the people that comprise it. For this reason they focus on making the people around them better. This is true in every walk of life. It is the reason why some athletes always seem to make the highlights early in the season, while others always seem to win championships in the end.

Make increasing your ability and the ability of team members a priority. It will increase both the individual and collective ability of team members, and the ability of your team to win in the end.

The greater part of progress is the desire to progress.
—Seneca (quoted in Roberts, 121)

Have the Courage to Seek and the Wisdom to Receive Wise Counsel

There are two ways to acquire wisdom; you can either buy it or borrow it. By buying it, you pay full price in terms of time and cost to learn the lessons you need to learn. By borrowing it, you go to those men and women who have already paid the price to learn the lessons and get their wisdom from them.

—Benjamin Franklin

Learn how to listen to and receive instructions from others. Access to the greatest minds, mentors, and books will be useless to you, unless you are coachable. Even if you are the best in your field, you will fall far short of your potential if you are not coachable. If you want to take advantage of the wisdom of others without the years of mistakes that usually accompany years of experience, take the following steps:

1. *Overcome your success*
   Success breeds comfort, comfort breeds complacency. Effective leaders know that what got them there doesn't keep them there. The day potential leaders stop growing is the day they forfeit their potential, and the potential of their organization.

2. *Swear off shortcuts*
   The longest distance between two points is a shortcut. As you desire to grow in a particular area, fig-

ure out what it will really take, including the price, and pay it.

3. *Trade in your pride*
Pride focuses on temporary appearances; being coachable focuses on permanent changes. The growth that results from being coachable will stretch your comfort zone. Not a temporary move out of your comfort zone, but a permanent change in the size and shape of your comfort zone. Being coachable requires us to admit we don't know everything, and to learn new things. The likelihood of mistakes grows as we grow. For the prideful, public mistakes are their: Goliath, their Jordan River, their point of no return, it is their Rubicon, their great divide, and their song that never ends. For the coachable it is their "turning point," their "launching pad," their "aha moment," and the resting place of their defeated foe. Trade in your pride.

4. *Never pay twice for the same mistake*
An old African proverb states, It is the fool's sheep that break loose twice.

Personal growth determines your preparation and your philosophy. Your preparation and your philosophy determine your attitudes and your associations. Your attitudes and your associations determine your activities and choices. Your activities and choices determine your results.

Most people start in the middle and then wonder why they aren't living their dreams. They focus on the results and spend time repeatedly floundering in activities that don't bring the desired results. Their focus is misplaced.

If you have the right activities, the right results will take care of themselves. But you won't have the right activities if you are unprepared and don't have the right philosophy. You can create the right philosophy through personal development, or you can continue doing what you've been doing, and keep getting what you've been getting. The choice is yours.

> *Success depends on previous preparation, and without such preparation there is sure to be failure.*
> —Confucius

Surviving Success

For leaders the problem with success is success. The higher you move up, the more disciplined you must be in ensuring that you learn from outside sources and hear conflicting views. This is more difficult than it sounds, because success brings a certain degree of seclusion and a proliferation of people who want or need to stay in your good graces. People who want or need to stay in your good graces will often be inclined to say what they think you want to hear. This makes it difficult to find people who will tell the emperor that he has no clothes on. Others assume that you are the boss, so you must be right. Even the most courageous teams, due to the insulation caused by efforts to protect their ideas or work product, may fall victim to groupthink.

As a leader, the more successful you are, the more susceptible you are to the mistaken belief that you have all the answers.

Each of the foregoing is a step off the precipice, for it means that you have stopped learning. While you have stopped learning, your competitors have continued learning. While you are pontificating to the market, your competition is listening to the market. While you are left wondering what happened to your market, your competition has walked off with your market. A personal growth plan helps leaders avoid these all-too-common pitfalls.

Christopher Ivan Franklin

You Will Be What You Believe You Will Be

*If you advance confidently in the direction of
your dreams, and endeavor to live the life which
you have imagined, you will meet with a success
unexpected in common hours.*
—Henry David Thoreau (quoted in *Live Your
Dreams*, 221)

It is difficult to achieve or maintain a level of success
any higher than what we believe we are worthy of. It is
not the chaos surrounding us that impedes us, but the
chaos characterized by self-doubt inside of us.

The better you feel about yourself, the more you expect of yourself. The more you expect of yourself, the
more you expect to succeed. The more you expect to
succeed, the more optimistic you are about the future.
The more optimistic you are, the more optimistic people you will attract.

Remember, winners are not attracted to whiners.
Your optimistic team of winners is more likely to see
and seize opportunity because that is what they expect
to see. The more opportunities seen and seized, the
more success you will enjoy. It is a self-fulfilling
prophecy that begins with how you feel about you.

*If you make a man feel that he is inferior, you do
not have to compel him to accept an inferior
status, for he will seek it himself.*
—Carter G. Woodson

128

Develop a Positive Self-Image

If you do not have a positive self-image, choose to change your mind regarding how you view you. When you change your mind, you will change your behavior, which will change your life. You may feel more comfortable seeking professional help. Such guidance is beyond the purview of this book, but there is a plethora of creditable books, guides, and professional organizations available for you to use as a resource. Take steps today to change those things that make you see yourself in a poor light. Consistent self-improvement is critical for ongoing self-approval. Do not accept somebody's negative perception as your reality. Take control of how you view you.

The first step is to assess yourself. Identify your strengths and weaknesses. If you cannot do this objectively, ask for help from someone who can. Begin to operate more in your strengths and compensate for your weaknesses. Map out a plan of disciplined study to acquire the life-changing skills you need to make your dream a reality. The daily practice of simple disciplines will do so much more for your self-image than you can imagine. Begin today.

You can't consistently perform in a manner that is inconsistent with the way you see yourself.
—Dr. Joyce Brothers (quoted in *Zig: The Autobiography of Zig Ziglar*, 105)

Christopher Ivan Franklin

THE FRANKLIN KEYS TO UNLIMITED POSSIBILITIES

6. Personal Development is the difference between possible and impossible.

Achieving a new vision requires a new level of accomplishment. A new level of accomplishment requires a new level of personal growth. Personal growth is the root of our lives. Success is the fruit of our lives. The condition of the roots determines the condition of the fruits. If you want to improve the fruits of your life, you must improve the roots of your life.

FRANKLIN KEY NUMBER 7: <u>MOVE FROM SUCCESS TO SIGNIFICANCE</u>

The key to realizing a dream is to focus not on success but significance...
—Oprah Winfrey (*O, The Oprah Magazine,* September 2002)

A life isn't significant except for its impact on other lives.
—Jackie Robinson (quoted in *The Right to Lead,* 47)

The highest level of success, in business and in life, is significance. To the extent that success is taught, the focus is overwhelmingly on getting. Significance comes only from giving. It begins when you inspire others to lead themselves. It is elevated when you influence others to lead themselves in areas of major significance despite the absence of any tangible benefit to you. It reaches its zenith when you are recognized as representative of the epitome of an ideal and others aspire to higher heights because of you.

You are significant, not because of who you are, or

even because of what you have achieved. You are significant because of what you represent in the lives of others.

Significant leaders add to the lives of others *and* multiply the qualities already there. Leaders of significance awaken some greater, but heretofore dormant, part of us. They emotionally and logically link/align the core values and aspirations of our best self-perceptions to the principles of a greater vision. They then issue a call to action, which, if acted upon, moves us from our current state to our desired state. They say, "Now," in the life of those they influence, where others, often the recipients themselves, say, "Later." Significant leaders exemplify what they teach. They walk their talk, and we are forever changed.

Significant people are not necessarily perfect people. Mother Teresa, Bill Gates, Martin Luther King, Jr., Mohandas Gandhi, and Jesus Christ quickly come to mind when thinking of leaders of significance. None of these people, with one obvious exception, was perfect, but few people would argue that they weren't significant. The achievements of these icons appear so far beyond the stratosphere that it is easy to see what they did but, in the glow of their achievements, miss *how* they did it.

Passionate Intent to Positively Impact Lives

I have a passion to positively impact your life by persuading you that you are endowed with the seeds of greatness . . .
—Zig Ziglar (*Over the Top*, ix)

Having a passion to positively impact the lives of others is the starting point for every great leader of significance. They may use different methods, but the intent, and the result, are the same. They intentionally lift those they lead. The single parent that sacrificed and taught the lessons that enabled the child to escape the noose of a pernicious environment is significant. The athletic coach that risks today's game by not playing a kid in order to teach a lesson that will last a lifetime is significant. The volunteer that gives her time to tutor a child, or to expand a child's vision beyond his daily existence, is significant.

Significant leadership is about leading through lifting and positively impacting the lives of others. A boss who demands performance solely for her own benefit will never be significant in the lives of those she leads. She may get compliance, but she will never get buy-in. Consequently, she may be driving, but she is not leading. There is a world of difference between the two.

You drive planes, trains, automobiles, and cattle, but you lead people. Drivers take; leaders cultivate. Drivers demand, based on authority; leaders affect through influence. Drivers ride others; leaders lift others. Drivers take the credit and assign blame; leaders take responsibility and give away the credit. Drivers are result-driven; leaders are result- *and* relationship-driven.

If you are unsure whether you are leading or driving, answer the question: Am I seeking to serve or be served? Drivers seek to be served. Leaders seek to serve.

Given equal or even slightly less talent, the team that is being led will, more often than not, have greater cohesion, commitment, creativity, and self-regulation; contribute beyond their individual "job descriptions" and ultimately outperform a team that is being ridden. The intent to positively impact lives is incompatible with driving people solely for selfish ends. Riding people is the antithesis of lifting people.

Leaders of significance have worked hard to achieve their success. But they also realize that they have benefited from the efforts of those who went before them. They in turn are passionate about being a benefit to others. They reach out to those behind them. Accepting them where, and for whom, they are, they then inspire them to aspire to greater heights. This is the mindset of significant leaders. They are passionately intentional about improving the lives of others.

Passion, zeal, enthusiasm, fervor are words of energy, of movement, of change. The energy created by passion is the force necessary to positively impact lives. While apathy and indifference do affect change, it is usually negative. Immediate positive change requires immediate positive energy. Positive energy is created by passion.

Leaders of significance cannot be apathetic or indifferent. They must be women and men of passion. Passion is evidenced by movement. Relentless movement undertaken in response to passion is the linchpin to greatness and the creator of energy. The force of passion enabled Mohandas Gandhi, in the days before TV, to influence 60,000 supporters to go to jail in nonviolent protest during the 1930s. His ideals precipitated the end of colonialism in the 1940s, the end of *de jure* American racism in the 1960s, and the end of South African apartheid in the 1990s.

Passion cannot be evidenced by talk; it must be evidenced by a walk, a behavior, an action. The overweight person on the couch at 11:30 PM with their feet up, enjoying the quart of ice cream, is not passionate about losing weight, but the lone man who stood in front of the tanks during the massacre in Tiananmen Square was passionate about freedom. If you want to be significant, you must be passionate.

Success is due less to ability than to zeal.
—Charles Buxton (Fuhrman, 142)

A Focused Passion

The passion of the significant leader is focused and unrelenting. Leaders of significance focus their energy, and they focus the energy of those they lead. Streams of light are powerful to the extent they are focused. Once focused, they are transformed from being merely pleasant into a powerful laser. Similarly, the time and attention of the leader of significance is powerful, to the extent it is focused. The leader's focus results in a consistency in language and behavior that impacts constituencies inside and outside of the leader's organization. To those outside the organization, it creates and projects the image conducive to the organization's goals.

Think about the first thing that comes to mind when people think of Walt Disney. Is it *Desperate Housewives*, or even ESPN? Of course not! It is either a Disney character or a Disney theme park. The Disney image is always of something clean, safe, and child-friendly, even though Disney is now the world's largest media conglomerate, with over $20 billion in annual revenue. Disney has unquestionably set the standard for image management.

Don't scoff at the idea of image management. Your image is what you look like in the minds of your potential clients and all you seek to influence. Their image of you may not be "true," but for better or for worse, the reality is, that image helps or hinders your success. It is not something the wise would leave to chance.

Focus has many benefits beyond the manner in which you or your brand is perceived in the public and private sphere. As the leader of a family, a team of two, or a team of 2,000, a focused leader empowers everyone on the team. Followers are empowered with the freedom and responsibility to act within the easily identified boundaries that focus and consistency establish. They are able to make decisions and trade-offs consistent with the organization's goals, even in the absence of specific instructions, and do not get bogged down waiting for instructions from on high, or evaluating endless options.

Martin Luther King's focus was on nonviolent civil disobedience. The training classes he conducted were on nonviolence. His speeches were on nonviolence. He won the Nobel Peace Prize because of his position on nonviolence. No matter what happened during the press for civil rights—attacks by the very police who had sworn to protect them; bombed homes; bombed churches; or murdered children—his followers knew that the only acceptable response was nonviolence.

Your stride to significance is accelerated exponentially when it is focused. The power and impact of focus is true generally, but has even greater impact in the context of significance. This is because significance is more often the result of impacting lives with a thought process, a philosophy, or belief, than about showing someone how to make a better widget.

If your behavior is capricious or inconsistent, it will be difficult for anyone to follow you, no matter how strongly they desire to do so. As every parent knows or will inevitably learn, "Do as I say, not as I do" doesn't work. What you do in private in front of your children will be repeated in public at the worst possible moment. This is true whether you are talking about children or employees. How you treat those who report to you is how they will treat those who report to them. How the so-called little people are treated is how they will treat your customers.

The best of the best are focused and consistent in their performance. The Three Tenors don't spend much time singing alto. *Phantom of the Opera, Cats, Les Misérables,* and *A Chorus Line* are the all-time longest-running shows on Broadway. Why? Was it because the endings changed from show to show? No, of course not! People liked the shows, recommended the shows, and went back to see the same shows, and the same endings, again and again. This is not to suggest that the significant leader must be inflexible, have a closed mind, or be unwilling to adapt to change. To the contrary, any leader that suffers from those afflictions will not be leading very long.

Motorola had 60% of the cell phone market locked down when it stubbornly chose not to respond to the demand for digital phones. Nokia at that time had only 11% of the market. Nokia chose to respond to the demand for digital phones. Motorola chose to ignore the winds of change, and the demands of its customers. Four years later the companies had roughly an equal share of the market. Today, Nokia is the leading cell phone provider, and Motorola's percentage of the market is hovering in the mid-teens. The cost to Motorola, its employees, and the thousands of employees it laid off as profits shrunk is easily in the hundreds of millions of dollars.

Leaders must change, but unless you stand for something, you cannot be significant in anything.

Charisma

A charismatic leader has the ability to relate the mission of the organization to deeply rooted values, ideals, and aspirations shared among followers.
—Jody Hoffer Gittell

All leaders of significance are charismatic. Often the image that comes to mind when we speak of a charismatic person is someone who is so smooth that they can sell ice to an Eskimo in the winter; radiates sunshine at midnight; has model good looks; always has it all together; and is every person's dream date for their child. But the reality may be a little different.

What is it that makes a gruff, overweight football coach such an icon to the grown man who, as a little boy, played for the coach? Why is the teacher who demanded the most of us the one we look back on with respect and fond memories? How is it that now when we remember the girl or guy in high school we thought was so cute, we think, *What a jerk*."!"

Former basketball coaches Dean Smith of the University of North Carolina and John Thompson of Georgetown University were not famous for being warm and fuzzy, or for suffering fools gladly. Yet, they are, without question, significant in the lives of hundreds of current and former players and coaches. When the men they have mentored speak of these former coaches, the basketball philosophies they were taught are secondary to the life philosophies that they learnt. So their charisma cannot be based solely on how they say what they say, but on how what they say touches those to whom they say it.

The Cost of Significance

America, undergirded by an ethos called the American Dream, is universally recognized, and unabashedly promotes itself, as the ultimate capitalist society. It is a dream that rests on the premise that everybody can play, anybody can win, and that to the winner goes the spoils, without limit. Names such as Rockefeller, Vanderbilt, Carnegie, Morgan, and Ford are the names in which the dream is encapsulated and held up to represent the possibilities available to all.

The idea that to the winner goes the spoils is no longer disputable. The most recent United States Government statistics show that the wealthiest 10% of households in America owns over 70% of the nation's net worth!!!

Beyond mere general statistics, in America we keep an annual running score. We track the billionaires separately from the millionaires. We track old money separately from new money. We track the CEOs who earn the most, and we even track the dead celebrities who earn the most. Those who attain phenomenal amounts of wealth are revered.

There is no national holiday in the United States that honors a person for what they have acquired. It is always in honor of what they have given. This is not as ironic as it may at first appear. It simply shows that even in America, where wealth is lionized, significance is not determined by how much you get, but how much you give.

Even the list of names generally recognized as epitomizing the American dream is not a mirror image of those who have made the most money. Nor is it a list of those who have been the most liked or loved. For all of these men have been alternatively loved and loathed from pillar to post. But what the list does reflect is an appreciation for those who, having gained substantial amount of wealth, gave substantial amounts back to society. These icons impacted the society in which they lived, and the one in which we live. We feel the impact of their lives and reap the benefit of their largesse, through such institutions as the Federal Reserve, the Metropolitan Museum of Art, Carnegie Mellon, the Carnegie Libraries; and the Ford Foundation. The philanthropy of these entities has impacted the entire world.

But the giving of millions is not the key to significance. If the giving of millions was the key to significance, few people would look into a TV camera and yell, "Hi, Mom." If the giving of millions was the key to significance, few people would be significant, for few people have millions to give.

Many have spent millions, in an effort to be significant, on what they thought to be a good cause. The millions spent on the war on poverty, drugs, and gangs have not eradicated poverty, drugs, or gangs. And those who spent the money are totally insignificant to the vast majority of those they said they intended to help. Millions are spent as countless people desperately seek to be significant in the lives of their children, spouse, or significant other. It doesn't work there either. But every successful parent, spouse, teacher, mentor, and volunteer will tell you, if you want to be significant in someone's life, the most important thing you can spend is your time.

Bridge the Gap

The difference between the haves and the have-nots is usually due to one of, or some combination of, the following: (1) knowledge; (2) relationships; and (3) will. There is absolutely nothing you can do for someone lacking the will to achieve. That door can only be unlocked from the inside. Even if you break the door down, they will not move. If you push them, they will only move as long as you are pushing hard enough to overcome their deadweight and their unwillingness. This is a waste of your time and energy. But don't lose heart. The story isn't over.

Two of the greatest tools man has ever thought of for transferring knowledge are Mr. Spock's "Vulcan mind-meld," and whatever allowed Neo to get "plugged in" then look up and say to Morpheus, "I know Kung Fu." For most of us, neither of these tools is in our repertoire. But there is something we can do.

One of the simplest and most incredibly powerful things we can do for others is to expose them to what we know. Not sell them. Not browbeat them. Simply expose them. Exposure without pressure gives them the freedom, security, and encouragement to dip into our pool of knowledge. This creates an interpersonal environment that allows us to help them to develop a taste, and ultimately a thirst, for knowledge. You don't have to push a person who has a thirst for knowledge. They are intrinsically motivated. Once you help a person to become intrinsically motivated to seek knowledge, you will have helped to change their life forever.

Too often, when asked about the development of their staff, some leaders will say some variation of, "If they want it, they will ask," or, "The information is available if they want it." This is a cop-out, and an abdication of responsibility. Leaders must initiate for the benefit of those they lead.

Beyond that, as a practical matter, few people know what they don't know. So how can they ask, or even have the desire, for that which they have no knowledge of? How can the untrained eye discern a diamond amongst the broken glass? How can you expect a person whose culinary highlights range from Wendy's to McDonald's to understand table etiquette or the proper use of cutlery? How likely is it that they will ask to be taken to dinner at Tavern on the Green, The Palm, or Windows on the World before it was destroyed on 9/11? They've probably never even heard of these places. How can you expect a child who has never been out of the inner city to appreciate the open vistas of the Midwest or the panoramic view of the Grand Canyon from a helicopter? They can't!!!

But you can help them gain an appreciation for what they don't know by exposing them to what you know. The idea is not to make sure that the child, or the adult, knows what you know, or see things the way you see things. That approach doesn't work when teachers and parents attempt to browbeat it into kids in school— How much algebra do you remember?—and it won't work here. The idea is to facilitate their learning through exposure and discussion then to assist them in relating to, and contextualizing the new ideas you are sharing with them. They won't grasp every idea that you share, nor will every idea understood be one they will gravitate toward. But having been exposed to more things, they are more likely to find some things that they do enjoy, that pique their intellectual curiosity, and ignite a desire for lifelong learning.

Social Trust

No man is an island, entire of itself....
—John Donne

Advancement in today's global society is predicated more on your social network (relationships) than on your social net worth (skills, education, personal attributes). Just as businesses need financial capital to be successful, people need social capital to be successful. Your network is your social capital. You need not even be aware of this network in order to reap its benefits. Numerous tests have been conducted where applicants with identical qualifications have been sent to apply for an apartment. Far too often the white applicant was treated differently than the black applicant.

In Washington D.C., in the days before the TSA (Transportation Security Administration) and their "random" security checks, two well-known newspaper reporters were traveling together on identical tickets issued through their newspaper. They were in the same line and were assisted by the same ticket agent. Yet, the black reporter was subjected to additional ticket confirmation procedures that the white reporter was not made to undergo. Women are usually charged more than men for the exact same cars, and usually paid less than men for performing the exact same job. The point is not the existence of discrimination per se, but that social capital engenders social trust. Social trust leads to opportunities and benefits that those outside of the real or perceived network are denied.

Significance Requires Sharing

There is no such thing as a self-made man.
—Anonymous

Most people understand the need and value of networks, but high achievers go a step farther and affirmatively cultivate their networks. One reason star performers in the workplace get more done than average workers is because they have better networks. Those outside of an effective network, irrespective of talent and effort, are at a disadvantage, compared to those operating inside of an effective network.

The immediate impact of an effective network can be seen live and in color during the course of a NASCAR race. To the uninitiated, NASCAR races appear to be a chaotic, every-man-for-himself, Darwinian survival of the fittest and fastest. But NASCAR has very stringent rules on car design and performance. All of the cars in the race operate under the same maximum speed limit, and across the board, the drivers and crews are the best in the world, so there is often little difference amongst the top teams and cars. Notwithstanding the NASCAR speed limits, the laws of aerodynamics enable the cars to go faster if they are lined up in what is called a "draft line." That is why the drivers seem to spend most of their time lined up behind each other during the race, and why it always seems that the car outside of the draft line is slowing down as the whole line passes them.

The draft line is analogous to an effective network.

Those running inside the network get a noticeable boost. A car running outside of a draft line is analogous to people attempting to compete outside of an effective network. Even though they have equal or greater talent, opportunity, and willpower, they will be overtaken by those inside of an effective network. The power of draft lines is so palpable that winning a major NASCAR race is predicated on the ability of drivers to suppress their competitive inclinations, and create temporary partnerships in order to harness the benefits of draft lines. Drivers, who know and trust each other, even if they don't like each other, create partnerships off and on throughout the race. Drivers who are new, not trusted, or simply disliked have a much harder time creating temporary partnerships while traveling at close to 200 mph.

Throughout the course of life, there is a significant boost given to those operating within effective networks. The competition to get into great schools starts in pre-kindergarten. Children have a better chance of getting into an upper-echelon private grade school if one of their siblings is already attending the school. Students stand a better chance of getting into an Ivy League school if one of their parents is a graduate of that school.

The need for, and the benefits of, an effective network continues after the formal education process is completed. There are many immensely talented, hardworking people and small companies that are not experiencing success commensurate with their abilities because they are operating outside of an effective network, that would excel far beyond their current status if given an opportunity to do so. Leaders of significance, from every walk of life, are intentional about playing key roles in providing those opportunities.

To the music fan, Janis Joplin, Pink Floyd, Carlos Santana, Chicago, Billy Joel, Bruce Springsteen, Blood, Sweat, and Tears, Luther Vandross, Whitney Houston, and Dido Armstrong represent vastly different genres and eras of music history. But even as the fortunes and popularity of these artists soared and soured, one thing linked them together. Music executive Clive Davis was significant in the lives of each of them. He either discovered them, signed them, or reintroduced them to the public after many years out of the spotlight, making it possible for them to live their dreams and for us to hear their music.

To the football fan, George Seifert, Mike Holmgren, Mike Shanahan, Ray Rhodes, and Dennis Green are successful current or former football coaches for various NFL teams. But Hall of Fame coach Bill Walsh was significant in each of their coaching careers, giving them the opportunity to work for him when they were young assistant coaches.

But you don't have to be a Hall of Fame football coach or a music industry icon to be significant in someone's life. You don't have to be a rich or famous hiring manager. This is well demonstrated in the life of "Big Jaz." Few people know or remember this recording artist who didn't make many records, didn't sell many records, and didn't make much money. But what he did do was expose another young man with a dream to the music industry. Having learned from the experiences of Big Jaz, the young man took a then untraditional approach to his own career. Today that young man is the part-owner of an NBA franchise, was the first non-athlete to have a signature line of sneakers, owns a successful clothing line, and has an estimate net worth of over $300 million dollars. The young man's name is Shawn Corey Carter, known to the world as Jay-Z.

Big Jaz was significant right where he was. You too can choose to be significant right where you are. Don't worry about what you don't have. Instead, use what you do have and be significant in someone's life. Your impact may go farther than you can imagine. People tend to do for others what was done for them. Consequently, when you share your knowledge and your relationships to impact someone's life, they are likely to do the same for someone else. Then you will be significant in starting a draft line that will impact lives for generations to come.

> *Your life should stand for something larger than your bank account, your personal achievements, and your successes.*
> —Christopher I. Franklin

THE FRANKLIN KEYS TO UNLIMITED POSSIBILITIES

7. *Move from Success to Significance*
    The highest level of success, in business and in life, is significance. You are significant not because of who you are, or even because of what you have achieved. You are significant because of what you represent in the lives of others.

THE FRANKLIN KEYS TO UNLIMITED POSSIBILITIES

1. *Self-Leadership is the Path to Greatness*

To achieve success you must lead others. In order to lead others, you must first lead yourself. Self-leadership requires the following: Play Your Game; A Vision; A Decision; Sacrifice; and Personal Development. To move from mere success to true greatness requires significance.

2. *Play Your Game*

In the game of life, whose game are you playing? Playing your game enables you to be strategic in your thinking and economical in your movements. If you are not playing your game, you are playing somebody else's game. Rarely is somebody else's game created for your benefit. If you want to win, if you want to achieve success and happiness, you've got to make up your own mind and play your game.

3. *Always Move Toward Your Vision*

To achieve great things, you must begin with a vision of the great thing you want to achieve. This empowers you to see things through the prism of whether it moves you toward, or hinders you from achieving, your dreams. It doesn't matter if achieving your dreams is going to take fifteen years. You are going to be fifteen years older in fifteen years anyway. Success begins with a vision.

4. *Make a Decision*

Successful people are successful because they decide to be successful. A vision without a decision to achieve it is worthless. Vision in the absence of a decision is customarily evidenced by an excuse why the vision cannot be achieved. Every decision must result in an action. If there is no action toward change, there was no decision to change. With your vision centered, and your decision made, the next step is to put together a plan, a road map of how to reach your goal. You must be definite about the goal, but flexible about the path to achieve it.

5. *Sacrifice*

Sacrifice is the price of success in any endeavor. The true indicator of how much you truly desire success is determined by the amount you are willing to sacrifice to achieve it. You will only be willing to sacrifice to the extent that the value of your vision is clear. The clearer you are about your desired end result, aka your vision, the more you will be willing to sacrifice to make it a reality.

6. *Personal Development Is the Difference between Possible and Impossible*

Achieving a new vision requires a new level of accomplishment. A new level of accomplishment requires a new level of personal growth. Personal growth is the root of our lives; success is the fruit. The condition of the root determines the condition of the fruit. If you want to improve the fruits of your life, you must improve the roots of your life.

7. *Move from Success to Significance*

The highest level of success, in business and in life, is significance. You are significant not because of who you are, or even because of what you have achieved. You are significant because of what you represent in the lives of others.

This is not the end. It is not even the beginning of the end. But it is, perhaps, the end of the beginning. —Winston Churchill (quoted in Collins and Porras, 201)

BIBLIOGRAPHY

1. Allen, James. *As a Man Thinketh*. Los Angeles: Tarcher, 2007.
2. Alva, Marilyn. "Condi Rice Rises to the Task: From National Security Adviser to Secretary of State, Condi Keeps Standing Her Ground," *Investor's Business Daily*, May 17, 2004.
3. Axelrod, Alan. *When the Buck Stops With You: Harry S. Truman on Leadership*. New York: Penguin, 2004.
4. Battelle, John. *The Search: How Google and Its Rivals Rewrote the Rules of Business and Transformed Our Culture*. New York: Penguin, 2005.
5. Bernstein, Peter L. *Against the Gods: The Remarkable Story of Risk*. New York: Wiley, 1996.
6. Blanchard, Ken, and Don Shula. *Everyone's A Coach*. Grand Rapids, MI: Zondervan, 1995.
7. Blanchard, Ken, Thad Lacinak, Chuck Tompkins, Jim Ballard. *Whale Done! The Power of Positive Relationships*. New York: Simon & Schuster, 2002.
8. Bloom, Harold. *Genius: A Mosaic of One Hundred Exemplary Creative Minds*. New York: Warner Books, 2002.

9. Brant, Martha, and Evan Thomas. "A Steely Southerner: Growing Up in Alabama Gave Condi Rice a Core of Strength. Just Ask the Russians; The Path to Power" *Newsweek*, Jan. 8, 2009, http://www.newsweek.com/id/76713.

10. Brinkley, Douglas. *The Unfinished Presidency: Jimmy Carter's Journey to the Nobel Peace Prize.* New York: Penguin, 1998.

11. Brown, Les. *It's Not Over Until You Win.* New York: Fireside, 1998.

12. ———. *Live Your Dreams.* New York: HarperCollins, 1992.

13. Bynum, Juanita. *Matters of the Heart.* Lake Mary, FL: Charisma House, 2002.

14. Carroll, Lewis. *Alice's Adventures in Wonderland.* New York: Penguin, 1961.

15. Collins, Jim and Jerry I. Porras. *Built to Last.* New York: Harper Collins, 1994.

16. Cooper, Robert K. *The Other 90%.* New York: Three Rivers Press, 2001.

17. Crocker III, H.W. *Robert E. Lee on Leadership.* New York: Random House, 1999.

18. D'Este, Carlo. *Patton: A Genius for War.* New York: Harper Collins, 1996.

19. Drucker, Peter F. *The Effective Executive.* Oxford, UK: Elsevier, 1967.

20. Felix, Antonia. *Condi: The Condoleezza Rice Story.* New York: Simon & Schuster, 2002.

21. Finkelstein, Sydney. *Why Smart Executives Fail.* New York: Penguin, 2003.

22. Fuhrman, John. *If They Say No, Just Say Next.* USA: Possibility, 1999.
23. Girard, Joe, Stanley H. Brown, Robert Casemore. *How to Sell Anything to Anybody.* New York: Warner, 1979.
24. Gitomer, Jeffrey. *The Little Red Book of Selling.* Austin, TX: Bard, 2004.
25. Goleman, Daniel. *Working with Emotional Intelligence.* New York: Bantam, 1998.
26. Gross, Daniel and Forbes Magazine Staff. *Forbes Greatest Business Stories of All Times.* New York: Wiley, 1996.
27. Harari, Oren. *The Powell Principles: 24 Lessons From Colin Powell Battle Proven Leader.* New York: McGraw-Hill, 2003.
28. Harvey, Eric, David Cottrell, Al Lucia, Mike Hourigan. *The Leadership Secrets of Santa Claus.* Dallas, TX: Walk the Walk, 2004.
29. Hill, Napoleon. *Think and Grow Rich.* Meriden, CT: Ralston Society, 1987.
30. Hoffer Gittell, Jody. *The Southwest Airlines Way.* New York: McGraw- Hill, 2003.
31. Janis, Irving L. *Victims of Groupthink: A Psychological Study of Foreign-Policy Decisions and Fiascoes.* Boston: Houghton Mifflin, 1972.
32. Kelley, Norman, ed. *R&B (Rhythm and Business): The Political Economy of Black Music.* New York: Akashic Books, 2002.
33. King, Charles, and James W. Robinson. *The New Professionals: The Rise of Network Marketing as the*

Next Major Profession. New York: Random House, 2000.

34. Landrum, Gene N., Ph.D. *Profiles of Female Genius: Thirteen Creative Women Who Changed the World.* Amherst, New York: Prometheas Books, 1994.

35. ————. *Profiles of Genius: Thirteen Creative Men Who Changed the World.* Amherst, New York: Prometheas Books, 1993.

36. Mair, George. *Oprah Winfrey: The Real Story.* London: Aurum, 1995.

37. Manz, Charles C. *The Power of Failure: 27 Ways to Turn Life's Setbacks into Success.* San Francisco: Berrett-Koehler, 2002.

38. Martin, Justin and Wayne Huizenga. "Wayne's World: Most entrepreneurs would be happy getting one company onto the FORTUNE 1,000. Wayne Huizenga has done it three times. Here's how." *Fortune,* May 12, 2003, http://money.cnn.com/magazines/fortune/fortune_archive/2003/05/12/342297/index.htm.

39. Maxwell, John C. *The 17 Essential Qualities of a Team Player.* Nashville, TN: Thomas Nelson, 2002.

40. ————. *The 17 Indisputable Laws of Teamwork.* Nashville, TN: Thomas Nelson, 2003.

41. ————. *The Journey from Success to Significance.* Nashville, TN: Thomas Nelson, 2004.

42. ————. *The Right to Lead: A Study in Character and Courage.* Nashville, TN: Thomas Nelson, 2001.

43. Mayer, Marissa Ann. "Turning Limitations into Innovation," *BusinessWeek* online, February 1, 2006, *http://blogs.zdnet.com/micro-markets/index.*

44. Miedaner, Talane. *Coach Yourself to Success*. Chicago: Contemporary Books, 2000.
45. O'Loughlin, James. *The Real Warren Buffett*. London: Nicholas Brealey, 2004.
46. Pulley, Brett. *The Billion Dollar BET*. Hoboken, NJ: Wiley, 2004.
47. Roberts, Wess, Ph.D. *The Best Advice Ever for Leaders*. Kansas City, MO: Andrews McMeel, 2002.
48. Russell, Bill, and David Falkner. *Russell Rules*. New York: Penguin, 2001.
49. Serwer, Andy. "It's iPod's revolution: We just live in it." *Fortune*, June 27, 2005, http://cnn.com/magazines/fortune/fortune_archive/2005/06/27/8263434/index.htm.
50. Simmons, Russell, and Chris Morrow. *Do You!* New York: Gotham Books, 2007.
51. Slater, Robert. *The Wal-Mart Triumph*. New York: Penguin, 2003.
52. Stone, W. Clement. *Believe and Achieve: W. Clement Stone's 17 Principles of Success*, rev. ed. Mechanicsburg, PA: Executive Books, 2004.
53. Thomas, Marlo, & Friends. *The Right Words at the Right Time*. New York: Atria, 2002.
54. Tracy, Brian. *Maximum Achievement*. New York: Fireside, 1993.
55. ———. *Victory!* New York: AMACOM, 2002.
56. Uldrich, Jack. *Into the Unknown: Leadership Lessons from Lewis & Clark's Daring Westward Adventure*. New York: AMACOM, 2004.
57. Vise, David A., and Mark Malseed. *The Google Story*. Macmillan, 2005.

58. Waterman, Jr. Robert H. *The Renewal Factor: How the Best Get and Keep the Competitive Edge.* New York: Random House, 1998.

59. Young, Jeffrey S., and William L. Simon. *Icon Steve Jobs: the Greatest Second Act in the History of Business.* New York: Wiley, 2006.

60. Zander, Rosamund Stone, and Benjamin Zander. *The Art of Possibility.* New York: Penguin, 2002.

61. Ziglar, Zig. *The Autobiography of Zig Ziglar.* New York: Doubleday, 2004.

62. ———. *Over the Top.* Nashville, TN: Thomas Nelson, 1994.